CAMBRIDGE

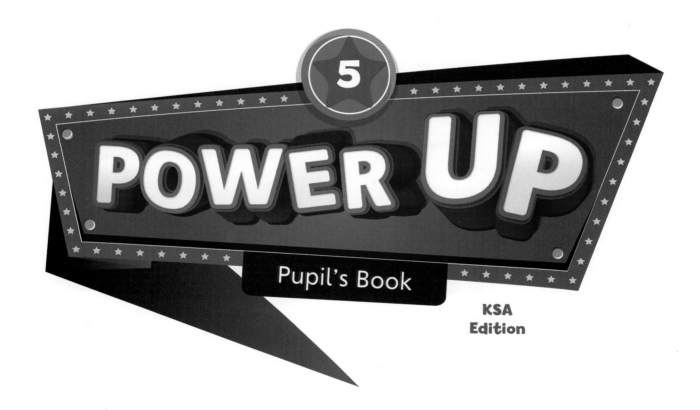

5

Power UP

Pupil's Book

KSA
Edition

Colin Sage

with Caroline Nixon and Michael Tomlinson

Map of the book

3

① In style

-20%

Which clothes can you see in the pictures?
When are the clothes used?

⭐ Mission Write a review

① Choose an activity and make a shopping list.

② Design an online clothes shop. Then swap shops and go shopping.

⭐ Write a review of the shop.

1 🎧 1.02 **Listen and point to the clothes. Then match the clothes (1–11) to the words in the box.**

> handbag   jumper   raincoat   suit   swimming costume
> tie   tights   tracksuit   trainers   jewellery   blouse

SEARCH

I love looking at clothes online, and here are some of my favourites. I'd love to get some of them one day … and it's my graduation soon!

1 You can put your phone in this.

2 Great for riding my bike in the park.

3 I ❤ this. It's warm and cosy!

+ make new board

4 You'll love 🌧 if you wear this coat.

5 Something for my brother (if he ever gets married?!?)

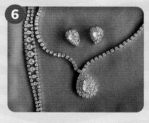

9 This is perfect to wear in spring.

6 This is beautiful – but more 💲 than some cars!

10 These are cute! And they look really comfortable.

7 My geography teacher wears this! It's awesome!!!!

11 These are cooler than a sunny day at the beach 🕶.

8 My favourite tennis player wears these!

2 **In pairs, read the sentences. Are they true for you?**

Mrs Fatima's wearing jewellery.

Mrs Fatima's wearing jewellery.
I've got a handbag at home.
I've got a swimming costume.
My teacher often wears a tie.

There's a raincoat in my bag.
I'm wearing a jumper.
My mum's got a tracksuit.
I'm wearing black tights.

No, she isn't.

I've got a yellow blouse.
There are trainers in my bag.
My dad's got a blue suit.

3 🎧 1.03 **PRONUNCIATION Listen and repeat.** page 118

1 Read Jim's blog and answer the questions.

1 What did Jim and Jenny want?

2 What were the problems with the things they bought?

3 What is a shopping fail?

Jim's Big Blog

Online Shopping Fails

22nd March @12:25 pm

Last week, I bought a T-shirt online to wear at my friend's graduation. I found a few websites where you can write on T-shirts. On one site, the T-shirts weren't as expensive as on other sites, and they looked nicer too. My friend is learning Spanish with me so I asked for 'Congratulations' in Spanish on the T-shirt.

The T-shirt arrived more slowly than I hoped. In fact, it arrived a few minutes before my friend's celebration. I put it on as quickly as I could, then I left to go. The T-shirt felt great – it wasn't bigger or smaller than I wanted.

When I arrived, I showed the T-shirt to my friend and he started laughing. I was confused – but then he told me about the problem with my T-shirt. It didn't say 'Felicidades' on the back. It said, 'Congratulations in Spanish'! 😱

At first, I was angry – but my friend said that the T-shirt made him happy. Then I felt a lot better. 😊

SHOPPING FAIL

22nd March @12:45 pm

Last month, I made an online shopping mistake that was as bad as Jim's.

My feet are growing quickly so I needed a bigger pair of trainers. I looked at two different websites. On the first site, the shoes were much more expensive. But on the second site, I saw a pair of shoes I loved – they were bright red and they were very cheap.

My mum ordered the trainers for me but when they arrived, I was surprised. The box was very small. Then, when I opened the box, I was shocked. The trainers were a lot smaller than my feet. And they were smaller than my toes too! In fact, they were trainers for a doll! 👟 What a mistake!

Now, I always check the size of the things I buy online.

2 Read the blog again. Who says each sentence – Jim or Jenny?

1 'My old ones are too small.'

> I think Jenny says this.

2 'Great! I love the colour and they're not expensive.'

3 'Wow! This is really comfortable.'

4 'This is awful! I look so silly.'

5 'That's strange. Why's this so small?'

6 'I'm happy it made you laugh.'

⭐ Grammar look: comparative adjectives, adverbs and *as … as*

'The trainers were a lot smaller than my feet.'

'On the first site, the shoes were much more expensive.'

'Last month, I made an online-shopping mistake that was as bad as Jim's.'

1 What is bigger? **the trainers** / Jenny's feet

2 Where did the shoes cost more? **on the first site** / on the second site

3 Whose mistake was worse? Jim's / **they were similar**

4 With short adjectives (one or two syllables long), we make comparisons with **-er than** / *more … than*.

5 With long adjectives (three or more syllables long), we make comparisons with -er than / **more … than**.

6 We use *as … as* to say something is the same or **similar** / different to something else. For example: 'I took the T-shirt out of the box as quickly as I could.'

7 We use *not as … as* to say something is similar / **different** to (and usually less than) something else. For example: 'The T-shirts weren't as expensive as on other sites.'

page 120

1 Make sentences to compare the pictures.

The tracksuit isn't as old as the trousers.

Did you know?

In the 1860s, some dresses were as wide as doors. Women often got stuck when they walked between rooms!

⭐ Mission Stage 1

Choose an activity and make a shopping list.

Hiking
a warm jumper, a cosy hat, trainers, a raincoat, trousers

My bag: 0 items   Register/Log in   Search

Vintage Online

Look cool fast with clothes from the past!

Search by year >

Search by item >

Price: £295
Size: medium; made in the 1860s

Price: £25
Size: extra large; made in the 1990s

Price: £295
Size: small; made in the 1970s

1 1.05 Match the sentences (1–7) to the clothes (A–G). Then listen and check.

1 It's made of **cotton**. It's got a picture of the sun on it.

It's got gold buttons.

The dress.

2 It's made of **leather**. It looks good for cold weather.

3 It's got a blue **collar** and it's made of **silk**. It's got gold **buttons**, too.

4 It's got a parrot **pattern**. You wear it round your neck.

5 There's a small **size** and a large **size**. You use them when you go walking.

6 It's got long **sleeves** and it's got a price **label**. It costs £25.

7 It's got a **chain**. There's a crocodile on it, too.

2 ⭐ In pairs, talk about what you like wearing at the weekend.

3 🎧 1.06 Listen to Safi and Rav packing. Do they need winter or summer clothes?

EXAM TIP! Write times as numbers (for example, **12:15**) not words (for example, quarter past twelve).

4 🎧 1.07 ⭐ Listen again. Complete the timetable.

School trip timetable

Tuesday:	Airport bus leaves at: **(1)** 6:15
Flight:	10 am–9 pm
Wednesday:	go to the **(2)** _____
Thursday morning:	shopping
afternoon:	**(3)** _____ at the hotel
Friday:	go **(4)** _____
Saturday:	whale watching at **(5)** _____

⭐ Grammar look: the present simple with future meaning

> When does the bus leave?   At 6:15!

1 What tense is the question? **present simple** / *going to* future
2 What time is the question talking about? **the present** / **the future**

3 The present simple is used to talk about timetables (for example, for buses, for lessons at school or for a holiday) in the **future** / **past**.

page 120

1 Put the words in order.

1 flight / When / does / leave? / the
_____

2 Where / start? / does / the / trip
_____

3 does / tour / Where / the / finish?
_____

4 is / time / dinner? / What
_____

5 the / day / What / farewell event? / is
_____

2 Choose one of the school trips. Ask and answer the questions from Activity 1.

1
Windsurfing in Spanish seas
- Flight leaves at 5:30.
- Start and end in Barcelona.
- Dinner is at 6 pm every day.
- There is a film every Saturday at the hotel.

2
South African Safari
✈ @ 8 pm Cape Town (trip starts and ends in Johannesburg)
🍽 7:30
🎉 Saturday

3
Trekking at the Edge of the World
We leave the hotel at 10 pm

Start and end in Riyadh

Dinner: 6:30

Farewell: Friday evening

⭐ Mission Stage 2
Design an online clothes shop. Then swap shops and go shopping.

1 **Look at the pictures. Which sentences do you think are true?** Read and check.

- The story is about places to go on holiday.
- The boy gives people advice on what to wear.
- The boy goes to a restaurant one day.
- The boy's plans are spoiled because of the weather conditions.

🎧 1.08

What NOT to wear!

I wrote a blog for my website last week about what clothes people should wear on different occasions. I know how frustrating it can be when you're invited to an event and there are important details missing from the invitation. For example, should you take a present? What time should you arrive? And (most importantly, I think) *what should you wear?* Wearing the right clothes has been a big problem for me in the past.

I got invited away for the weekend with a friend and his family last year. I thought we were going camping in the mountains, so I packed all my warm clothes – my thick woollen jumper, my coat and scarf, and a hat to keep my head warm. I was prepared for the cold nights sleeping in a tent by a lake. So, imagine how I felt when we arrived at the beach! I had no swimming costume or towel, and no light clothes! My friend lent me some swimming shorts and I had to buy a cotton T-shirt and some light trousers because it was so hot during the day. I had a great time, but I wish my friend had told me that his family had changed their plans. He completely forgot!

Another time, my friend Hakim invited me for a meal. I was surprised when I arrived and met Hakim outside the restaurant. He was wearing a smart shirt, trousers and shiny shoes. I was dressed in jeans and trainers! Apparently, it was a special dinner because Hakim's older brother had just graduated. His whole family were there – parents, grandparents, aunts and uncles … I thought we were getting a pizza or something, but it was a really fancy restaurant and all the waiters were wearing ties! Luckily, I had time to run home and change before the rest of his family saw me through the window.

That's why I wrote my blog last week. I wouldn't want that happening to anyone else.

Text type: a realistic story

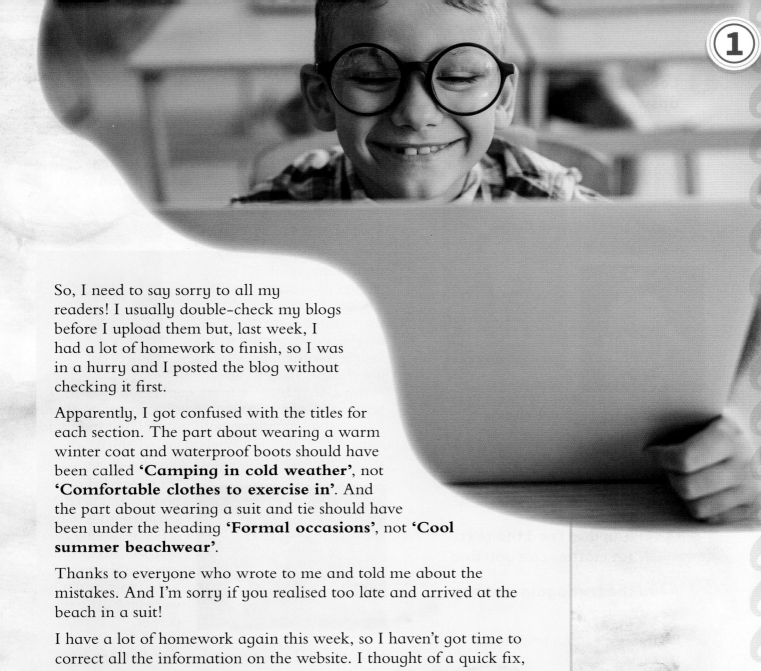

So, I need to say sorry to all my readers! I usually double-check my blogs before I upload them but, last week, I had a lot of homework to finish, so I was in a hurry and I posted the blog without checking it first.

Apparently, I got confused with the titles for each section. The part about wearing a warm winter coat and waterproof boots should have been called **'Camping in cold weather'**, not **'Comfortable clothes to exercise in'**. And the part about wearing a suit and tie should have been under the heading **'Formal occasions'**, not **'Cool summer beachwear'**.

Thanks to everyone who wrote to me and told me about the mistakes. And I'm sorry if you realised too late and arrived at the beach in a suit!

I have a lot of homework again this week, so I haven't got time to correct all the information on the website. I thought of a quick fix, though: I've changed the title of the blog from **'What to wear'** to **'What NOT to wear!'** I hope everything's clearer now.

2 **In pairs, talk about the questions.**

1 Do you think the boy knows about what clothes to wear for different occasions?

2 Why didn't the boy wear the right clothes when he went out with his friends?

3 What was the problem with the boy's blog entry? Why did it happen?

4 How did the boy solve the problem?

5 Imagine you turned up at an event wearing the wrong clothes because you read the boy's blog? What would you write in a letter to him after the event?

1 Look at the pictures and answer the questions.

1   When did people wear these clothes?

2   What do you think the clothes are made of?

3   Which styles do you like the best?

2 🎧 1.09 Listen and read the text. What clothes can you find?

3 Read the text again and say *yes* or *no*.

1   Everyone could wear silk in the Middle Ages.

2   Cotton is a manmade textile.

3   You need 25 plastic bottles to make a fleece.

4   Fleece is better for the planet than wool.

5   Smart textiles can change shape.

4 In pairs, talk about the questions.

1   Which materials is your shirt made of?

2   How do you think we will use smart textiles in the future?

Clothes in the past

In the past, people used natural materials to make their clothes like animal fur and skin. They also used leaves and plants. In the Middle Ages, most people wore warm woollen clothes, which came from sheep. Shoes were very simple and they were made of leather. Only very rich people could wear silk and colourful clothes, as dyed fabrics were expensive.

What we wear today

Today, we still use many natural materials for our clothes like cotton, wool, silk and leather. We also use manmade textiles, like acrylic, polyester and nylon. People like them because they are cheaper than natural textiles. They have different qualities too – swimwear is made of manmade materials because they dry faster. Our clothes often have both natural and manmade materials. Check the label on your T-shirt!

Fleece is a very special, manmade fabric. It's made

from recycled plastic bottles. You need 25 plastic bottles to make a fleece sweater or a blanket! Fleece fabric keeps us warm, it's waterproof and it helps us to look after the planet.

What will we wear in the future?

In the future, we could all be wearing smart textiles. These clothes have little sensors hidden inside and they catch energy from our body. They can change colour, light up and even grow. Smart textiles are important for sport. For example, a T-shirt could help keep a football player cool during a match. Smart textiles can also be fun. Imagine your friends' faces when your T-shirt suddenly changes color!

Did you know?

In Europe in the Middle Ages, they didn't make shoes for the left and right feet.

1 Match the text types in the box to the examples A–D.

> a short email   a note
> an advert   a notice

A

Clean clothes as fast as a car!

Two shirts for the price of one!

B

Sara,

Don't wash your clothes in the washing machine. It broke this morning. You can use the sink in the kitchen.

See you later,

Mum

C

IMPORTANT NOTICE

PLEASE TAKE OFF YOUR SHOES BEFORE YOU ENTER SECURITY

D

Dear Bill,

We change your towels daily and clean your room every morning after breakfast.

We hope you have a great time!

Janet Mills

(Manager)

2 **Look at the texts again.** Match the titles (1–4) to the texts (A–D).

1 Hotel information _____

2 A machine that doesn't work _____

3 Airport information ___C___

4 A special offer _____

3 **Read the text and answer the questions.**

> George,
>
> Uncle Bob will be here for dinner tonight. Please buy him a nice present after your lessons. He loves funny ties!
>
> Dad

1 What kind of text is it?

_____

2 Who wrote the message?

_____

3 What does George need to do?

_____

4 When should George look for a present?

A at dinner time

B before school

C after school

1 🎧 1.10 📝 **Listen and match.** Put the pictures in the correct order.

> I've marked your test and I've got some good news!

> That's E.

A

B

E

C

D

2 🎧 1.11 **Read the questions and look at the pictures.** Which words will you hear? Listen and check.

1 Why can't Karen help her mum?

A

B

C

2 Which trainers does the boy take?

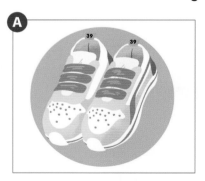
A

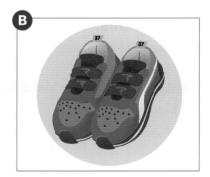
B

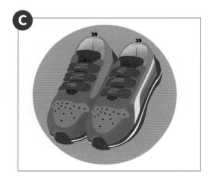
C

3 🎧 1.12 **Listen again and choose the correct answer.** Why is this correct?

EXAM TIP! Use the **first** listening to choose an answer. You can check your answer the **second** time you listen.

1 Complete the sentences.

1 My jumper is old, but my tracksuit is older.

My jumper is newer than my tracksuit.

2 The red raincoat is expensive, but the blue one is more expensive.

The blue raincoat is more _____ .

3 My raincoat is smart and so is my suit.

My raincoat is as _____ .

4 My cotton socks are comfortable and so are my silk ones.

My cotton socks are as _____ .

5 My old jumper is big, but my new jumper is bigger.

My old jumper is smaller _____ .

2 Complete the sentences. Use the correct form of the words in the box.

| finish   open   leave   start   close   arrive |

1 When does the toy shop _____ again? At 9 am tomorrow.

2 When does the bus _____ ? In fifteen minutes.

3 What time does the film _____ ? At 12:30.

4 The school _____ after lunch on Saturday.

5 The play doesn't _____ until 8 pm.

6 The train _____ in two hours.

⊛ Mission in action!

● Say what activity you had to buy clothes for.

● Say why you chose the shop.

● Write a review of the shop.

3 Choose ten words from this unit. Record the words using the steps below.

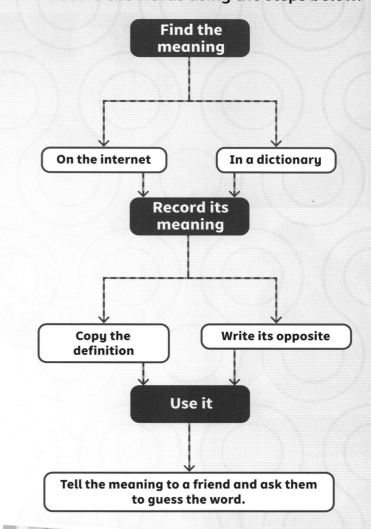

Find the meaning

On the internet   In a dictionary

Record its meaning

Copy the definition   Write its opposite

Use it

Tell the meaning to a friend and ask them to guess the word.

We wanted to buy clothes. So we chose Jana's Boutique.

The silk blouse was the correct size and colour. The order arrived in perfect condition. I can recommend this online shop for smart clothes. ★★★★★

Mission Recommend new technology

Is the technology in each picture useful? Why? Which would you like to use the most?

① Find the class's technological needs.

② Show how a piece of technology works.

⭐ Present your group's best option.

1 🎧 1.13 **Listen, point and say the numbers.**

> 🎧 x.x This is my laptop. I use it …

> Number 4.

2 **Match the words in the box to the numbers 1–10 in the picture.**

> software   disc   hardware   laptop
> screen   mouse   printer
> computer program   keyboard   mobile phone

> Number 8 is software.

3 📝 **Look at the words in Activity 2 and complete the challenges.**

1 Find the six kinds of hardware.
2 Write a sentence that uses the words 'disc' and 'program'.
3 Find three things that turn on and off.
4 Name three pieces of computer software.

1 **Look at the poster.** What can you see? What would you like to look at?

Look! There's a robot.

2 🎧 1.14 **Listen to Tom talking to a friend about a technology show.** What does Dale want to look at?

TECHNOLOGY SHOW TODAY
King Abdullah Cultural Center, Al Jubail

3 🎧 1.15 ⭐ **Listen again.** Match the people (1–5) to the objects (A–H).

 **1** Sam

 **2** Dale

 **3** Brian

 **4** Chris

5 Scott

 **A** mobile phones

 **B** laptop

 **C** keyboards

 **D** screen

 **E** digital printer

 **F** mouse

 **G** software

 **H** robot

4 🎧 1.16 **PRONUNCIATION Listen and repeat.** page 118

EXAM TIP! Remember that there are **three options** that aren't used.

⭐ Grammar look: the first conditional

'If my mum says it's OK, then I'll go.' | **1** Will Sam's mum say it's OK? **Yes / Maybe**

2 We use the first conditional to talk about things that **might / won't** happen.

page 120 →

1 **Which sentence is correct? Choose A or B.**

1 **A** If my mum says it's OK, I'm going to the park this weekend.
  B If my mum says it's OK, I'll plant some tomatoes tonight.

2 **A** I get a new hat if it's not too expensive.
  B I'll buy a new keyboard if it's not too expensive.

3 **A** I'll have fun if I join the school basketball club.
  B I'll have fun if I'll play video games tonight.

4 **A** Kim will email her aunt if she finishes her homework in time.
  B Chris goes too if he finishes his homework in time.

5 **A** If I go to the fair, I'll see all my friends.
  B I go to the school play, I'll see all my friends.

6 **A** If I go to the fair, I'll look at the robots.
  B If it rains, have to stay inside.

2 **Complete the sentences. Use your own ideas.**

1 If my mum says it's OK, _____ .
2 _____ if it's not too expensive.
3 I'll have fun if _____ .
4 _____ if she finishes her homework in time.
5 _____ I'll see all my friends.
6 If I _____ , _____

3 **In groups, share your sentences. Who wrote the most interesting sentence?**

I'll have fun if this toy helicopter flies!

I'll have fun if I play games on my brother's tablet after school.

⭐ Mission Stage 1

Find out the class's technological need and choose your group's favourite!

What do you think we need in our classroom?

I think these tablets help us to learn a lot!

Tablets ✓✓✓
Laptop ✓

1 Read the school webpage. Who has a robot that gives food to cats? _____

| M | 🔍 Wall \| Find friends \| Chat \| Profile |

JIM

Hi friends,

How will computers be different in 10 years' time? How will they help us? I'm making a poster about the future of computers and need ideas!

Thanks

Jim

In 10 years' time, I think there will be lots of computers in our homes. In fact, I think that we'll **chat** to computers all day.

The computers will help us a lot. If I'm hungry, I'll ask the freezer, 'What ice cream have we got?' Or if I take photos, I'll ask my phone to **upload** them to my blog.   – lbcat2

In 10 years' time, I think we'll stop using mice. Instead, we'll control our computers using our bodies. When we want to **click** on something, we'll close one eye. And, when we want to **download** a game or a film, we'll look down at the floor.

If we want to **turn on** a computer or **turn** it **off**, maybe we'll jump in the air!   – CoolJen

If a computer has a small problem, like a broken 'enter' key, people often throw it away. But in the future, computers will be easier to repair. Maybe we'll be able to **install** programs or borrow robots that repair our computers? And if our computers break, they'll be easy to recycle.   – SolSky

My uncle's got lots of robots. If the floor is dirty, a robot drives around and cleans it. Another robot feeds his cats if they're hungry and **texts** his mobile phone when he needs to buy more cat food!

In 10 years' time, the computers in robots will be able to do almost anything. They'll help us by writing **emails** and doing our homework!   – Jungles17

2 🎧 1.18 Match the icons (1–9) to the words in bold on the webpage. Then listen and check.

1 is 'chat'.

3 Read the webpage again. Who says each sentence?

1 'My friends and my sister are helping me with a project.'

I think Jim said this.

2 'Before I go outside, my cupboard will tell me if I need an umbrella.'

3 'Computers in the future will be easier to fix.'

4 'In the future, we'll be able to install programs by smiling.'

5 'In 10 years' time, a computer will be able to make Jim's poster for him.'

4 Say sentences with the words from Activity 2.

I chat with my friends online on Saturdays.

★ Grammar look: the zero and first conditional

'If the floor is dirty, a robot drives around and cleans.'

1 When the floor is dirty, how likely is it that the robot will clean? **Yes, the robot will clean. / Yes, the robot might clean.**

2 What kind of sentence is this? **Zero conditional / First conditional**

'If I'm hungry, I'll ask the freezer, "What ice cream have we got?"

3 Will the boy be able to talk to the freezer in the future? **Yes, he will. / Yes, he might.**

4 What kind of sentence is this? **Zero conditional / First conditional**

5 We use the first conditional to talk about things that might happen. We use the zero conditional to talk about things that are **never / always** true.

page 120

1 **What do you do now and what will you do in the future? Ask and answer.**

1 Your computer doesn't turn on.
2 Your keyboard's 'enter' key is broken.
3 You want to chat to your friends.
4 You want to download a game.
5 Your floor is dirty.

At the moment, if my computer doesn't turn on, I ask my dad to help me.

In the future, if my computer doesn't turn on, I'll be able to repair it on my own.

2 **Write notes about how computers will be different in 10 years' time. How will they help us?**

★ Mission Stage 2

Show how your piece of technology works.

If you install this program, you can practise your English.

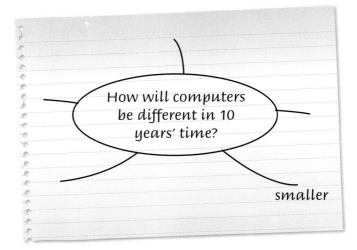

How will computers be different in 10 years' time?

smaller

1 **What are the most popular newspapers in your country? Does your school have its own newspaper or news section on its website?**

THE TIMES

1.19

If it happens, we write about it

Friday 28th May | No 134

RANYA WINS!

The winner of The King Abdulaziz City for Science and Technology Design-an-app Competition surprised everyone. Malik Ahmed tells us what happened.

This Monday, there was a surprise winner of Dr Hussein's Design-an-app Competition. Ranya Ali, who only joined the Academy last month, won first prize for her brilliant Timetabler app, which helps students organise their time.

Dr Hussein announced the competition at the beginning of May. She said, 'The app must be easy to install and use on a mobile phone, and it must help students with their schoolwork. It shouldn't use lots of battery.' Throughout the month, this newspaper followed the competition. We spoke to students about possible winners and everyone said the same thing: 'If Fawzeya Hassan enters it, she'll win it.' 'Fawzeya knows everything about computers,' said Sama Mahmoud. 'Her parents teach her.' 'She'll be the Steve Jobs of Jordan one day,' said Latifa.

Everyone was surprised when Dr Hussein announced the winner of the competition. Ranya Ali is new to the school and very quiet. Nobody knew that she designed her first app when she was only seven years old. Now she is the star of the software class and everyone wants to talk about her app. 'It makes it easy to plan your time!' said Ola Khalil. 'I love it!' said Isa Khatib.

'With Ranya's app, I can make a timetable really quickly!'

PROFILES

Name: Fawzeya Hassan
Age: 11
Interests: chess, reading

Name: Ranya Ali
Age: 11
Interests: video games, photography

Text type: a newspaper article

Although Fawzeya was disappointed when she lost the competition, some students say that she and Ranya are going to design a new app together. If that happens, you'll be able to read all about it in the *Times*.

AN INTERVIEW WITH THE WINNER

What does your app do?

RANYA It makes a timetable for students.

Can you explain that?

RANYA Of course! You tell the app what exams you need to study for. You also tell it when the exams are. Then you click on the special 'plan' button and the app makes a timetable for you.

Do you mean it tells you what to study and when?

RANYA Yes, that's right! That means you have more time for studying because the app does the planning for you.

Technology Fact of the Week

Have you ever consulted a robot for medical advice? Well, in Saudi Arabia you can do exactly that. Robotics specialists created a way that people visiting Hajj can find hospitals and doctors all over the country. They stand in front of a robot that shows a screen and can consult in real time with specialists of all kinds!

2 **In pairs, role play a conversation.** Imagine you are Ranya and Fawzeya.

STUDENT A You are Ranya. You feel happy because you won the competition. You have lots of ideas for new apps. Ask Fawzeya if she would like to help you design a new app.

> I can't believe I won!

STUDENT B You are Fawzeya. You feel disappointed because you wanted to win the competition. Ask Ranya about her app.

> Can I ask you some questions about your app?

1 Which apps do you use? What do they do?

2 Listen and read the text. What do these numbers mean?

2 million $1 million   400 million

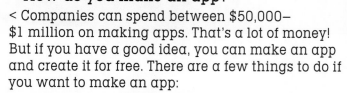

< What's an app? >

< There are lots of apps that you can download to a smartphone or laptop. The most popular are games, news, weather and social media apps. If you have an app on your phone, you just have to click on it. This means you don't need to search for a program or write the address of a website. One of the first apps was a game called 'Snake'. Players had to make a line of dots around the small screen. This might not sound very interesting, but 400 million people played this simple game. Now there are over 2 million apps to choose from. >

< How do you make an app? >

< Companies can spend between $50,000–$1 million on making apps. That's a lot of money! But if you have a good idea, you can make an app and create it for free. There are a few things to do if you want to make an app:

1   Think about what your app is going to do, how it will be good for the people using it and how you will let people know about your app. Write your ideas on a piece of paper and draw pictures.

2   Go online and check if there are other apps like yours. If there are, how is yours better?

3   Wireframe your idea. A wireframe is like a storyboard. You draw your design idea so that you can see what your app does. There are lots of different wireframing websites to help you do this.

4   Learn the language of app building. Lots of schools have coding clubs, which teach you the languages you need to build apps. You need to choose a coding language and learn the rules. For example, when you are using HTML5, you need to use these symbols < > at the beginning and end of your codes. >

3 In pairs, talk about about the sentences. Say *yes* or *no* and why.

1   I'd like to play 'Snake'.
2   I'd like a maths app.
3   I think making an app is easy.
4   I'd like to make my own app.

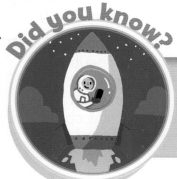

Did you know?

A mobile phone is more powerful than the computer that sent astronauts to the moon in 1969.

1 Match the question words with the phrases. What information should the answer have?

What …?	A thing
Where …?	A time
Who …?	A place
When …?	A short description
Tell me about …	A person

2 Match the questions (1–6) to answers (A–F).

1 What's your family name?

2 Where are you from?

3 What do you like about your school?

4 Where did you go on holiday last year?

5 Who usually cooks in your house?

6 Tell me something about a new hobby you would like to try.

A I'm from Seville but I live in Madrid.

B It's Bowring.

C My family and I went to Corfu in Greece.

D It's got a big gym and a modern computer room.

E When I finish my exams, I'll start a short course on writing programs for computer games.

F My parents usually do the cooking but my brother is quite good at making curries and desserts!

3 In pairs, ask and answer the questions.

Hello, I'm Sally. Can I have your mark sheets please? Thank you.

What's your name?

I'm …

Do you like clothes shopping?

Yes, I go with … I like to buy …

Where do you go at the weekend?

I go to the …

What's your favourite subject at school?

I like … and … . Oh, and … of course!

When do you watch films?

On … I usually … with my friends.

Where do you usually have lunch?

Sometimes … but I often …

Tell me something about your family.

Well, I've got …

EXAM TIP! Try to **speak clearly** and remember to give **as much information** as you can!

1 **Do the quick quiz.**

1   What is a blog?

    a   a sauce   **b**   an animal
    c   something to read

2   Who can write a blog?

    a   anyone   **b**   children
    c   adults

3   Where can I read a blog?

    a   in a comic   **b**   online
    c   in a book

2   **In the exam, you read about three people talking about the same thing. You have to decide which person says something. What do you think is the best way to do this?** Choose and put the sentences in order.

A   read each text once   **C**   choose a letter

B   read the questions   **D**   read the three texts again

_____ _____

3   **Choose the correct answer.**

1   Which person doesn't write as much as before?

    a   Now I'm nineteen and I don't write my blog very often.

    b   I post a message once a week.

2   Which person sometimes gets a message they don't want?

    a   … sometimes I get emails from my school.

    b   Sometimes I get a strange message on the screen but I don't mind … I just delete it immediately!

3   Which person was the youngest when they started their blog?

    a   I started my blog when I was thirteen.

    b   I started blogging when I was twelve.

4   Which person needs some help to write their blog?

    a   My computer is so slow! Sometimes I need to ask if I can use my brother's.

    b   When the wifi is broken, I can't post a new blog.

EXAM TIP! Don't worry if you see some words which you don't know. You will still be able to answer the question.

① Match the sentence halves.

1. If the laptops are cheap, …
2. If I can't go to the park, …
3. If I want to do my homework on a computer, …
4. If you press 'enter', …
5. If her keyboard is broken, …

A the program will download.
B I'll chat to my friends online.
C I'll buy a new one today.
D Grandma won't be able to email me.
E I'll need a printer.

② ⭐ Read the email. Choose the correct answer.

Hi Jim,

Sorry for replying so slowly!

At the moment, when you order pizzas, they often **(1)** _____ slowly. When there **(2)** _____ a lot of traffic, the pizza can get cold too! In the future, I think that flying robots will carry pizzas. So **(3)** _____ you want one, it will be at your house in less than five minutes. **(4)** _____ you want the pizza cut up, the robot **(5)** _____ do that for you too!

– Mike

1. A arrive   B arrive   C arriving
2. A was   B will   C is
3. A while   B because   C if
4. A When   B Can   C Are
5. A able   B will   C is

EXAM TIP! Read the text **once** to understand it. Then read the text **again** and choose the best word for each space.

⭐ Mission **in action!**

- Present your group's ideas.
- Choose the best new technology for the class.

③ Look at the new words from this unit. Make puzzles with the words using the steps below.

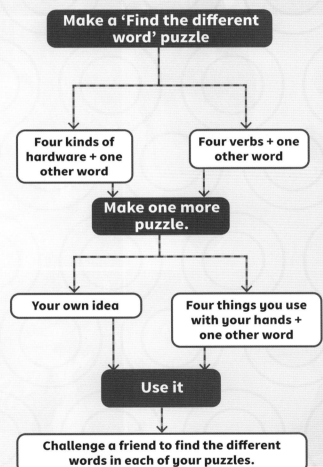

Make a 'Find the different word' puzzle

Four kinds of hardware + one other word

Four verbs + one other word

Make one more puzzle.

Your own idea

Four things you use with your hands + one other word

Use it

Challenge a friend to find the different words in each of your puzzles.

This is a great new …

3 Jim-nastics

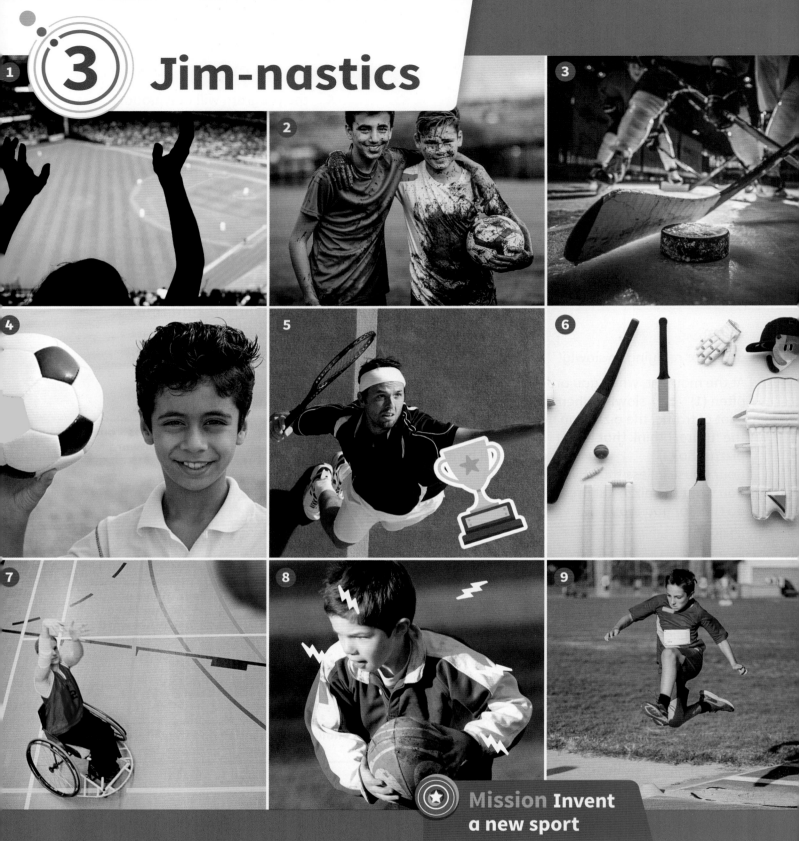

What sports can you see in the pictures?
Which of the sports is your favourite?

★ **Mission Invent a new sport**

1. Make a mind map to compare sports.
2. Invent and describe a new sport.
★ Play the sport and vote for the best one!

28

1 🎧 1.21 **Read the TV guide.** Match the words in blue to the pictures below. Then listen and check.

Rugby is number 7.

Wednesday, 9 October				
	7:00	**7:30**	**8:00**	**8:30**
Sport 1	Rugby tonight: Wales vs. Australia		Deep diving: Daniel swims with sharks	
Sport 2	Small white ball: Exciting golf from around the world		Cricket chat: A review of today's cricket matches	
US Adventure	Cycling: A man, his bike and America's biggest mountains	Ice-hockey special: See the skaters on the ice for Russia vs. Canada		Surfing: Hawaii's best surfers surf the ocean's biggest waves
FIT1	Be fit boxing: Get your gloves on and get fit	Gymnastics at home: Jump and stretch with Paul	Be fit boxing: Get your gloves on and get fit	Gymnastics at home: Jump and stretch with Paul
AllStars	Sports stars of tomorrow: Watch athletics stars run, throw and jump to prepare for the Olympics		Snow idea: Snow skiers try water-skiing for the first time on Lake Tahoe	

2 Write the sports.

Sports I've tried: _____

Sports I've not tried but would like to try: _____

Sports I just want to watch on TV: _____

3 ⭐ **Do you like the sports in Activity 1? In pairs, say why or why not.**

I love cycling. I go every week with my dad and my brother. It's a great way to see the countryside. Do you like cycling?

EXAM TIP! Be ready to help your partner by repeating what you say or asking them questions.

For example:

Why don't you like …?

What do you think about …?

How about …?

1 **Read Jim's blog.** What animal's actions do zorbers copy?

Jim's Big Blog

If you think that sports like golf or gymnastics aren't interesting enough, you might want to try something a little stranger. I've found three really unusual sports to tell you about.

The world's three strangest sports

The Mud Olympics

The Mud Olympics is held every year in a small German town called Brunsbuettel. Around 50 teams from different countries meet and play football and other sports in deep mud. As you can see, the players get very dirty! Yuck! There are lots of prizes – and people love playing in the mud – but the main reason that the event is arranged is to get money to give to charities.

Man versus Horse

This athletics event is held in Llanwrtyd Wells in Wales. At the event, men and women race a horse for 35 kilometres. People often think that the horse will win easily – but the race is planned so that the horse and runners finish at nearly the same time. How's that done? Well, there are lots of mountains near Llanwrtyd Wells and horses are very slow at going down hills!

Zorb Racing

Zorbing started as a fun hobby, where a person climbs inside a giant blow-up ball – the zorb – and rolls down a hill for fun. Now zorbing is also practised as a sport. Competitors race zorbs across tracks, fields, and even water. The zorb is moved forward by the person inside, who uses their arms and legs to roll the ball, like a hamster on a wheel. It can be a bumpy ride, but an exciting one!

2 ⭐ **Read the sentences and choose the correct event.**

	The Mud Olympics	Man vs. Horse	Zorb Racing
1 People copy how an animal moves.	A	B	C
2 Groups do the event together.	A	B	C
3 The event happens in an area where there are lots of hills.	A	B	C
4 People collect money at the event.	A	B	C
5 Competitions happen in many different places.	A	B	C
6 The person or animal who finishes this event first is the winner.	A	B	C

EXAM TIP! Focus on the **general meaning** of the text and don't worry if there are some words that you don't know.

⭐ **Grammar look:** the passive (present simple)

'The race is planned so that the horse and runners finish at nearly the same time.'

'The zorb is moved forward by the person inside …'

1 Who plans the races in Man vs. Horse?
We don't know / The runners

2 Who moves the zorb forward?
We don't know / The person inside the zorb

3 Which word says who controls the zorb?
the / by

We use the passive when we **(4) know / don't know** who does something or when it **(5) is / isn't** important who does something.

page 121

1 **Complete the sentences.** Use the words in brackets and the passive in the present simple.

How to plan a zorb racing competition

Ideas for the zorb racing event **(1)** _are discussed_ (discuss). Plans **(2)** _____ (make) to be sure that the event is safe.

The zorbers meet and the event starts. The winner of each competition **(3)** _____ (give) a prize – it could be a trophy in the shape of a zorb!

Photographs of the event **(4)** _____ (take) and **(5)** _____ (share) on the internet.

Zorbs **(6)** _____ (collect) and litter **(7)** _____ (clean) from the site.

⭐ **Mission Stage 1**

Make a mind map to compare your feelings about different sports.

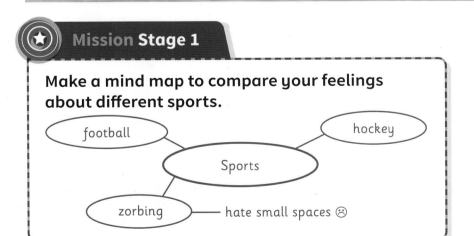

2 **In pairs, say sentences and say which sport it is.**

It's held every year.

The Mud Olympics.

Yes!

1 🎧 1.22 **Listen. Match the sports commentaries (1–4) to the photos (A–D).**

A ☐ B ☐ C ☐ D ☐

2 🎧 1.23 **Match the definitions (A–K) to the words (1–11). Listen and check.**

1 ☐ goal
2 ☐ coach
3 ☐ train
4 ☐ surfboard
5 ☐ net
6 ☐ hit
7 ☐ racket
8 ☐ court
9 ☐ cyclist
10 ☐ track
11 ☐ helmet

> 1 is J.

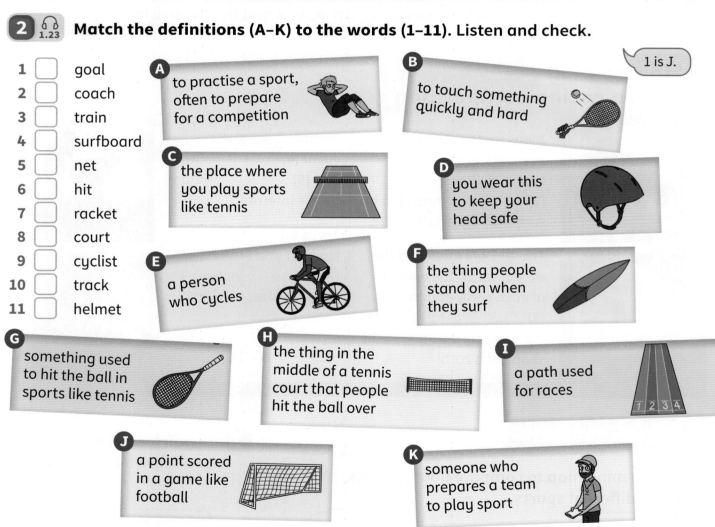

A to practise a sport, often to prepare for a competition

B to touch something quickly and hard

C the place where you play sports like tennis

D you wear this to keep your head safe

E a person who cycles

F the thing people stand on when they surf

G something used to hit the ball in sports like tennis

H the thing in the middle of a tennis court that people hit the ball over

I a path used for races

J a point scored in a game like football

K someone who prepares a team to play sport

3 🎧 1.24 **Listen again. Why are the numbers below important?**

three minutes | 2–1 | 35 minutes | $1 million | one point | two metres | ten | eight

★ Grammar look: modal verbs

'Birch may have made a mistake.'

'This could be the most important point today.'

'The Silver Beach surfing competition will start in about 35 minutes.'

'Hugh hits it back well but the ball might go into the net!'

'Can Habib shoot?'

'Shall we watch that goal again?'

1 Modal verbs **are** / **aren't** followed by the infinitive form of a verb without 'to' (e.g. *speak, go, walk* etc.)

2 When you use *he* or *she*, you **do** / **don't** need to add an 's' to the modal verb.

3 To make a question, you **do** / **don't** change the order of the modal (e.g. *might, will, can* etc.) and the subject (e.g. *I, you, he, she* etc.).

4 There **are** / **aren't** *-ing* forms of modal verbs.

page 121

1 🎧 1.25 **PRONUNCIATION Listen and repeat.** page 118

2 Read the dialogue and choose the correct words.

3 Act out the dialogue. Then act it out again, changing the underlined words.

4 Choose a sport and write a short sports commentary. How many modal verbs can you use?

Harley
online

(1) Shall we / We shall <u>play tennis</u> tonight?

Yes, **(2) would I / I'd like to**. But <u>it's cloudy outside. It may rain.</u> 😲

If it rains, we **(3) can / might** <u>play table-tennis inside</u>.

Great! 😃

Could you **(4) to bring / bring** <u>balls</u>, please?

I don't have any. But I can ask my brother. He **(5) might / shall** be able to <u>lend us some</u>.

OK. I'll see you later then.

See you later!

We're here at the lake to watch the water-skiing today, and we might be lucky with the weather …

★ Mission Stage 2

Invent and describe a new sport.

1 **Look at the pictures.** What do they show? How is the story told?

🎧 1.27

The injured champion

'What an interesting tennis final here at the Athens Open, with team second, Stefanos Andino, taking over from injured champion, George Demitriou, at the last moment.'

'Absolutely! George is sitting by the side of the court holding his crutches as Stefanos serves against Italian opponent, Marco Russo.'

'I wonder how George is feeling as he watches his teammate stand where George should be today.'

'I imagine in a lot of pain because of that fractured ankle, but also some emotional pain at seeing this opportunity taken away from him. It's no secret that George doesn't think Stefanos is ready to take on Russo.'

'Do you think that's a genuine opinion from George, or is it because of the rivalry between these two players?'

'Maybe both. Apparently, yesterday, George tried to share some advice with Stefanos about technique, but Stefanos wasn't interested in listening to his teammate.'

'Yet here's George at the side of the court watching the match. I guess he doesn't give up so easily.'

'Russo wins another point! It looks like George was right after all. Stefanos is having a bad game so far. And George doesn't look happy. He's standing up and shouting something at Stefanos. Careful, George. You don't want to damage that ankle even more!'

'By the look of George's hand gestures, he's telling Andino to stand further back from the net. But once again, Stefanos Andino ignores him. He obviously wants to play his own game.'

'And another point to Russo! I think it's time Stefanos started listening to his injured teammate.'

'Look, George is standing up again. What's he saying to Andino now?'

'It looks like he keeps telling Andino to stand further back. That way, he has a better chance to reach the longer shots, but he's close enough to the net to hit back the short balls.'

'Well, John, you used to be a professional tennis player. Is he right?'

'Absolutely. But will Andino pay attention? George has been trying to convince him the whole match and Andino isn't interested. You have to admire George's perseverance. He's doing everything he can to help his teammate.'

'Well, that perseverance might have finally paid off. Stefanos is further back now and … yes, he's won the point. Now another short ball from Russo and Andino steps forward and … he reaches the ball!'

'A tense moment as Stefanos Andino serves to win the final game in this set. He serves, runs forward. George shouts something. Andino

hears him, bounces to the right, and moves close to the net. He barely reaches the ball, but … knocks it over the net and Russo misses the return shot. Stefano Andino, with the help of his injured teammate, wins the set for Greece!'

'George leaps up, drops his crutches, and hops on one leg as Andino runs over to him and supports him before he falls over. Now that's teamwork!'

2 In pairs, talk about the questions.

1 How do you think George felt about not being able to participate in the tennis final?

2 What kind of person is George? How did this help Stefanos win the match?

3 What was the relationship like between George and Stefanos?

4 How does their relationship change at the end of the story? What action shows how their relationship has changed?

1 **Look at the pictures.** How do these activities help you to prepare for a sports competition?

2 🎧 **1.28** **Listen and read the text.** How many hours a day does each athlete train?

Every four years, the Olympics is shown on TV. It takes years of training and hard work to compete at an Olympic Games and there are many things that an athlete has to think about before they run around the track, hit a ball or put on a helmet for that important race.

Gymnasts

Training: Gymnasts train for six hours a day. As well as this, they swim, cycle and run to make their legs stronger. It's important that they stretch every part of their body before and after they practise or they might get injured.

Food: Gymnasts need to eat a lot of protein (chicken and fish) and healthy snacks like bananas and strawberries.

Rest: They have one rest day a week and try to get a good night's sleep too. It's difficult to train if you are tired.

Greek gymnast Eleftherios Petrounias is the 2016 Olympic champion and three-time World champion (2015, 2017 and 2018).

Sprint hurdlers

Training: Sprint hurdlers train in a similar way to sprinters.However, they also practise running in shorts bursts, which they repeat over and over. This improves endurance, speed and power each time they land after a jump and then continue their sprint.

Food: Endurance athletes need a lot of protein in their diet, like eggs, beans, nuts, fish and meat. Carbohydrates, like pasta, oatmeal and potatoes, are also important to balance their diet and help provide fuel. During workouts and competitions, a sprint hurdler should drink eight ounces of water every 20 minutes and eight ounces of special sports drinks every hour. They contain electrolytes to help hydration.

Rest: Sprint hurdlers should rest for up to 96 hours after an intense training session or competition so that the body can recover completely. Athletes often train hard one day and follow an easier routine the next. Running on grass and at lower speeds can help to improve general fitness and recovery after a particularly intense workout.

 Hadi Soua'an Al-Somaily made history when he won a silver medal for the 400 metres hurdles at the Sydney Olympics in 2000 – the first athlete to win an Olympic medal for Saudi Arabia!

3 **Read the text again and answer the questions.**

1   How often can you watch the Olympic Games?

2   What do athletes need to do before competing?

3   Why should athletes stretch before and after training?

4   Why is strength training important for runners?

5   Why do hurdlers practise repeated running over short distances?

6   Write examples of each of the food groups:
     Protein: …   Carbohydrates: …

1 🎧 1.29 **Look at the example answer and listen. What will the children learn?**

Surf Camp
When: _Summer_

2 🎧 1.30 **Match the correct type of information (1–7) to the words in bold. There are two extra answers. Listen and check.**

1 A food   5 A time
2 A place   6 A name
3 An age   7 A body
4 A price   part

A   Surfing might look hard and your **stomach** might hurt …
B   Your gym coach is Bob Vanya, that's **V-A-N-Y-A**.
C   Half of your food needs to be water, **fruit** and vegetables …
D   We think **45** minutes a day is enough!
E   If you want help choosing your meals, I'll be in the Main **Hall** …

3 🎧 1.31 **Listen again and write the correct answer in the gap.** Use the words in bold from Activity 2.

Camp

When:	_Summer_
Food:	(6) 50% water, _____ and vegetables 50% meat and sugars
Help with meals:	(7) Main _____ after 6 pm
Use gym:	(8) After every lesson for _____ minutes
Name of coach:	(9) Bob _____
First day:	(10) _____ might hurt.

EXAM TIP! The answer could be a **word** or a **number**. You may also need to **spell a name**.

1 **Read the text and answer the questions.**

1 Who is Billy? 〔 Billy is Henry's friend. 〕
2 Where is he?
3 What sport is he doing?
4 Who is he writing to?

From: Billy   **To:** Henry

Hi Henry,

How **(1)** _are_ you? I'm trying a new sport called cricket. It's not like baseball but it's very popular here **(2)** _in_ India! I've got **(3)** _a_ great coach. He's called Kishan and before he became a coach he played in a famous **(4)** _team_ .

Yesterday, our group practised in the park. Kishan showed **(5)** _us_ how to hold the bat and hit the ball. Later, Mum and I watched a match. Kishan **(6)** _was_ playing with his new team and they won! Afterwards, Kishan said I could keep the ball!

I'll send you **(7)** _some_ photos after my lesson.

Write to me soon!

Billy

---

2 **Look at the underlined words in Activity 1.** What type of words are they?

- verb
- indefinite article
- preposition
- pronoun
- auxiliary verb
- noun

3 **Complete the email.** Use the words in the box.

〔 went   I   my   the   for 〕

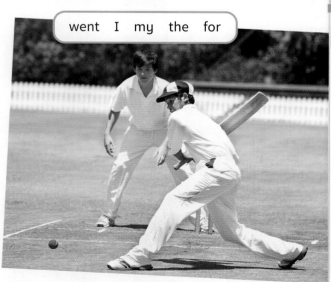

From: Henry   **To:** Billy

Dear Billy,

Thanks **(1)** _____ your message. Cricket sounds like a lot of fun.

I'm on holiday with **(2)** _____ family in Sri Lanka, which is near India. We **(3)** _____ cycling this morning and then I took my surfboard to **(4)** _____ beach in the afternoon.

Talk soon!

Henry

---

1 **Rewrite the sentences in the passive. Don't use the underlined word.**

1 <u>People</u> hold The Mud Olympics every year.
   The Mud Olympics is held every year.

2 <u>People</u> play lots of different sports.

3 <u>People</u> play football.

4 <u>People</u> sell tickets to the football game.

5 <u>Someone</u> gives prizes to the winners of the competition.

6 <u>People</u> need lots of showers at the event.

2 **Write the sentences in the negative and question form.**

1 You can play cricket well.
   You can't play cricket well.
   Can you play cricket well?

2 I could hit the ball.

3 You should train every day.

4 We can go water-skiing here.

5 I may get a surfboard from that shop.

6 I will play ice hockey.

3 **Choose ten words from this unit. Record the words using the steps below.**

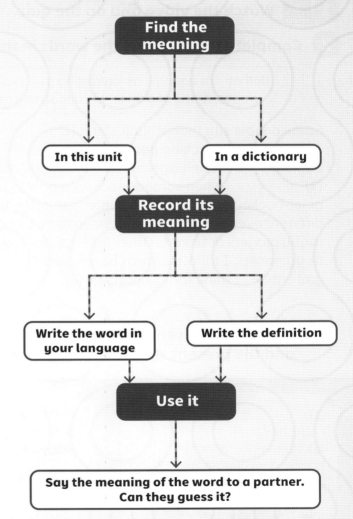

Find the meaning

In this unit — **In a dictionary**

Record its meaning

Write the word in your language — **Write the definition**

Use it

Say the meaning of the word to a partner. Can they guess it?

Mission in action!

- Present the new sport.
- Play the sport and give tips.
- Vote for the best!

How to win at my sport:

- Don't forget a helmet! Then you won't be scared.
- You don't need to worry about the other players.

Review ●●● Units 1–3

1 ▶ **Watch the video and do the quiz.**

2 **Complete the text. Use the words in the box.**

> dull as   as boring   as interesting as   exciting as
> as strong and thin   big and strong as

Some people say that athletics isn't **(1)** _____ other sports.
They say that watching people run is **(2)** _____ as watching
paint dry. But I don't agree! The ends of athletics races are as
(3) _____ when someone scores a goal in a sport like football
or ice hockey. And, when you watch athletics, you see lots of
different events. Some athletes have to be as **(4)** _____
rugby players or boxers. Other athletes have to be **(5)** _____
as gymnasts. I think the most boring sport is cricket. I don't like
golf either – I think that's nearly as **(6)** _____ cricket.

3 **Complete the sentences. Use the words in brackets
and the present simple with future meaning.**

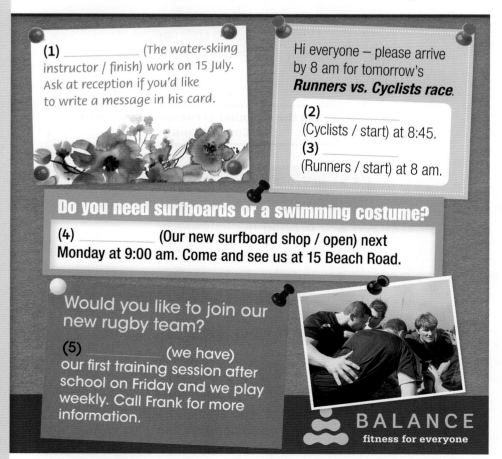

(1) _____ (The water-skiing
instructor / finish) work on 15 July.
Ask at reception if you'd like
to write a message in his card.

Hi everyone – please arrive
by 8 am for tomorrow's
Runners vs. Cyclists race.

(2) _____
(Cyclists / start) at 8:45.
(3) _____
(Runners / start) at 8 am.

Do you need surfboards or a swimming costume?

(4) _____ (Our new surfboard shop / open) next
Monday at 9:00 am. Come and see us at 15 Beach Road.

**Would you like to join our
new rugby team?**

(5) _____ (we have)
our first training session after
school on Friday and we play
weekly. Call Frank for more
information.

BALANCE
fitness for everyone

4 **Complete the text.**

(1) ___If___ it's sunny at the
weekend, I **(2)** _____
go shopping with my
friend, Sue. We'll go to the
town centre and look in
the shops. There are holes
in my jumper's sleeves, so
(3) _____ there's a
sale, I'll buy a new one.
(4) _____ get one
with a cool pattern,
(5) _____ I can
find a pattern I like.
Sue wants to buy a
leather handbag – I think
(6) _____ buy one if
it's not too expensive.

5 📝 **What are you
going to do this
weekend? Who
will you spend
time with? Write
25–35 words.**

6 Say six sentences.

If	+	you like the tracksuit you get brown leather shoes it snows later my blouses are dirty my swimming costume is wet the jewellery isn't expensive	+	my mum will wear her raincoat. they'll look good with your brown trousers. I'll get a new gold chain. I borrow clean ones from my sister. you should try it on. I put it in the garden to dry.

7 Find the mistakes. Write the correct sentences.

1 My best friend it is called Luisa.

2 In my bedroom there's a bed which made of wood.

3 My favourite film is call **One Last Time**.

4 The school events are organised the teachers.

5 The food is choose by my cousin.

6 They eat special cakes which make for the wedding.

8 Choose the correct words to complete the sentences.

1 I **wouldn't** / **might not** like to chat to my favourite actor. I'm too shy.

2 Can you **download** / **downloading** these pictures for me, please?

3 Could you **texting** / **text** Grandma and ask her what time she's coming?

4 He **shall** / **might** email me after dinner.

5 **I may** / **May I** turn on the TV, please?

6 **Shall I install** / **Install I shall** this software for you?

9 Choose and complete two of the challenges.

CHALLENGE 1

Look at Unit 1. Find three:
- things people wear when they exercise.
- parts of a shirt.
- things people wear over shirts.
- things clothes are made of.

CHALLENGE 2

Look at Unit 2 pages 17 and 20. What are five things your computer has got? What are five things your computer can do?

CHALLENGE 3

Find a sports word in Unit 3 that starts with each of the following letters:

B-I-R-D-W-A-T-C-H-E-R-S

4 Be careful!

What ways of staying safe can you see in the pictures?

Mission Find out about emergency services

1 Make a list of questions about the emergency services.

2 Find answers to your questions about the emergency services.

⭐ Present what you have found out.

1 🎧 2.02 ⭐ **Listen and choose the correct answer.**

1 The shark bit the man when he was …

A looking for a golf ball. **B** swimming. **C** feeding it.

2 The fire started because of …

A the X-ray machine. **B** someone cooking. **C** a candle falling.

3 The man with the big hands hurt himself when he was …

A using scissors. **B** preparing food. **C** playing in the park.

> **EXAM TIP!** Read the questions **before** the listening starts.

2 🎧 2.03 **Complete the sentences. Use the words in the box. Then listen and check.**

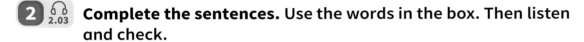

injured break appointment cut painful heart accident ankle emergency door patient

1 Yes, he _____ his hand when he was feeding a shark.

2 I've made an _____ for the man to meet the doctor.

3 What's wrong with this _____? The man who's having his _____ checked.

4 That woman's running to the _____. Do you know why there's a fire?

5 I think there was an _____ and the X-ray machine caught fire.

6 Did the woman _____ her _____ in the accident too?

7 While he was making a sandwich, his knife slipped and he _____ his hand.

8 It looks very _____. It must hurt a lot.

3 **In pairs, ask and answer about the picture in Activity 2.**

> What's wrong with this man?

> He's injured his hand.

1

VIKTOR, JIM

Hi Jim – how are you?   8:27

I haven't been well for a week.   8:27

Jared told me. Did you get our card?   8:28

Yes – thank you!   8:29

I want to come back soon though to see you all. But I feel awful!   8:29

Yeah, but you need to stay in bed if you want to get better. Drink lots of water!   8:30

I will.   8:31

Can't wait to see you again.   8:31

You too.   8:32

2

ELIZABETH, ALEXA

Hi Alexa – would you like to come to the park later?   7:04

No, sorry. I need to take my rabbit to the vet.   7:07

Oh no! What's wrong with her?   7:08

She's had a problem with her heart since April.   7:09

    7:10

Poor thing! I hope she's better soon.   7:10

Me too! The vet says that she'll be fine.   7:11

3

JULIAN, IAN

I've broken my ankle 😫.   4:21

I was playing tennis in the courts in the park when a cat ran towards me. I tried to get away by jumping over the net but I fell over it and broke my ankle 😨 😨 😨 😨.   4:21

Oh no! How long has your ankle been injured?   4:22

Since Tuesday. I've been at home since then.   4:22

Is it painful?   4:22

No, it's fine — but I feel very bored. I haven't left my house for days! 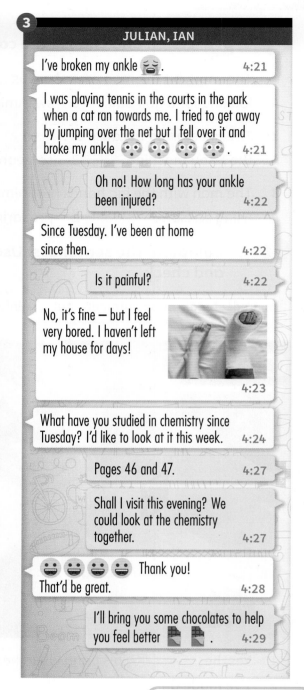   4:23

What have you studied in chemistry since Tuesday? I'd like to look at it this week.   4:24

Pages 46 and 47.   4:27

Shall I visit this evening? We could look at the chemistry together.   4:27

😀 😀 😀 😀 Thank you! That'd be great.   4:28

I'll bring you some chocolates to help you feel better 🍫 🍫.   4:29

---

1 ⭐ **Look at the messages again.** Choose the correct answer.

1 Why is Viktor writing to Jim?

A He's worried about his friend.   **B** He's going to get Jim a glass of water.   **C** He wants Jim to write a card.

2 Why did Elizabeth write to Alexa?

A Her rabbit is unwell.   **B** She's going to go to the vet with her.   **C** She wanted to go to the park with her.

3 What do Julian and Ian agree to do together?

A eat sweets   **B** study chemistry   **C** go to the park

> **EXAM TIP!** After you've chosen A, B or C, read the text and the question again to **check** that **your answer** is correct.

★ Grammar look: the present perfect with *how long*, *for* and *since*

'I haven't been well for a week.'

'She's had a problem with her heart since April.'

1 When did Jim start feeling unwell?
a week ago / **Monday**

2 Does the rabbit still have a problem? **Yes** / **No**

We use the present perfect to describe actions that started in the (3) **past** / **present** and are still happening in the (4) **present** / **future**.

With (5) *I*, *you*, *they* and *we* / *he*, *she* and *it* we use *have* + past participle (e.g. *made*, *done*, *eaten* etc.).

With (6) *I*, *you*, *they* and *we* / *he*, *she* and *it* we use *has* + past participle.

page 122

1 2.04 **PRONUNCIATION Listen and repeat.** page 118

2 **Write six true sentences.** Use the phrases in the box or your own ideas.

I haven't had a cold		a few hours.
I've lived in my house	for	three weeks.
		a month.
I haven't felt sick		five years.
		a long time.
I've been at this school		as long as I can remember.
I've studied geography	since	Monday.
		this morning.
I haven't eaten chocolate		23rd January.
		yesterday.
		last winter.
		I was born.

_____

_____

_____

_____

_____

_____

3 **In pairs, share your sentences from Activity 2. Who hasn't felt sick for the longest time?**

★ Mission Stage 1

Make a list of questions about the emergency services.

How can I call the emergency services?

Who will come?

What sound does an ambulance make?

Did you know?

A long time ago, when people had sore throats, they tried to get better by putting dirty socks around their necks. Some people put fish on their feet too!

1 **Read the diary. What happened to Lizzy at the lake?**

4th August

I'm excited because tomorrow I'm going to the hills with my aunt and my little sister, Lizzy. We're going to take a walk and then we're going to go swimming in a lake. We're not going home until after dinner!

My aunt's meeting us tomorrow at 9 am to drive us there – so I should go to sleep now. 😊

5th August

Today, something awful happened. We were having a lovely day in the hills – everybody was happy and we had a lovely picnic. But when we went to the lake, things started to go wrong.

We were swimming when Lizzy cut her leg badly on a rock. She fell over and started crying. We put a **bandage** round her leg and helped her back to the car.

It looks really painful so we're taking her to the doctor this afternoon. 🙁

6th August

The doctor gave Lizzy a **prescription** for some **pills**, and she said that Lizzy needs to have a small **operation**.

Also, I think I've got the **flu**. When I got out of the lake, I was so worried about Lizzy that I forgot to get warm and dry. My mum's given me some medicine for my headache. She told me to go to bed and rest. But when I **lie down**, I can't sleep because I'm worried about my sister.

7th August

I've got some great news. Lizzy's operation was a success! She's **resting** at the hospital at the moment and the doctor says she can come home tomorrow. Hooray!

I'm **feeling better** too. So I'll be able to help look after Lizzy when she gets home.

2 **Match the words in bold in the diary to the pictures below.**

Number 1 is 'resting'.

3 **Add one sentence (A–D) to the end of each day's diary entry.**

A   I wonder what she'll say.

B   I can't wait to see her again!

C   I hope her operation is OK.

D   I'm so excited about the trip.

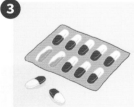

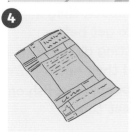
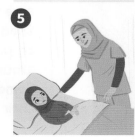

⭐ Grammar look: the present continuous for future plans

'We're taking her to the doctor this afternoon.'

'We're not going home until after dinner!'

1 When will Lizzy go to the doctor? **In the future** / now
2 Will Lizzy definitely go to the doctor? **Yes** (they've made the plan) / **No** (they'll make the plan this evening)

1 The present continuous can be used to talk about the present and the **past** / **future**.
2 The present continuous is used to talk about the future when something is **uncertain** / **planned** and we say when it will happen.

page 122

1 **Look at Jack's calendar.** Complete the sentences below using the present continuous.

My plans!

 today

	Sunday	Monday	Tuesday	Wednesday	Thursday	Friday	Saturday
	17	18	19	20	21	22	23
	6 pm – make cookies for my family	lunchtime – go to athletics club		after school – get Mum a present (not flowers!)	evening – do my maths homework	film the video diary	

1 At 6 pm today, Jack's making _____ .
2 _____ at lunchtime tomorrow.
3 _____ on Wednesday after school.
4 On Thursday evening, _____ .

> At 6 pm today, Jack's making cookies for his family.

5 On Friday and Saturday, _____ .
6 On Tuesday, _____ .

2 **In pairs, talk about your plans.** How many are the same?

… at 6 pm today? … tomorrow lunchtime?

What are you doing …

… on Wednesday after school?

… on Thursday evening?

… at the weekend?

What are you doing after school today?

I'm going to watch an ice-hockey match!

⭐ Mission Stage 2

Find answers to your questions about the emergency services.

Search   Emergency services contact 🔍
About 9,397 results (0.21 seconds)
What's the number for emergency services?

1 **Read the title of the story.** What do you think it's going to be about?

Koalas and crocodiles

Waleed's ill and bored. He has flu, and he has had a fever for several days. But today he's feeling a bit better. His mum says he can go downstairs, lie down on the sofa and watch television with his sister, Fatima.

Waleed and Fatima are watching a programme about crocodiles. There's a knock on the door. It's their cousin, Elyas. He has come to see if Waleed's feeling better. 'How long have you been ill?' he asks. 'For four days,' says Waleed. 'I haven't been to school since last Monday!' 'Lucky you!' says Elyas.

The crocodile programme has finished. The local news programme is starting. 'There was an incident at the zoo last night. A terrible storm knocked down a tree, and it broke the koala enclosure. A whole family of koalas escaped!'

'I know that zoo,' Fatima says excitedly. 'It's on the high street.' Waleed's feeling sleepy. His eyes are closing! 'Come on, Waleed,' says Elyas. 'Let's climb some trees.'

★ ★ ★

Outside in the garden, Waleed's climbing a tree, and Elyas quickly climbs up to join him. 'What's that noise?' Waleed asks, startled. 'I didn't hear anything,' says Elyas. 'Shhhhhh!' whispers Waleed. 'There it is again!' 'Oh,' says Elyas, 'I hear it now. Where is it coming from?' They both feel a bit worried. 'Look!' says Elyas. 'There!' 'What *is* it?' asks Waleed, now frightened.

One of the koalas walks towards the tree and looks up at the boys. 'It's a koala!' whispers Waleed. 'You know, one of the koalas from the zoo on the high street. Look! There's the whole family!' 'Yes, and look at the baby,' says Elyas. 'Don't scare them.'

The whole family looks up now as if startled. The children freeze.

The children watch in complete silence while the koala calms down, and then the whole family starts to walk away through the wood. 'Let's go!' says Elyas, climbing down the tree fast. 'Come on, Waleed,' he shouts. 'What are you waiting for? We have to save them.' But Waleed isn't feeling well. He thinks he might have a fever again. As he's climbing down the tree, he cuts his knee and cries out in pain.

Elyas walks towards the koala family. He makes so much noise that Waleed starts to feel nervous. They don't see the mother koala come up behind them and she looks furious. The baby koala looks scared. 'Don't,' Waleed shouts to Elyas. But Elyas grabs the baby koala and the mum is chasing him. They cross over the river. But Waleed can't run to the bridge. His knee's bleeding. It's too painful to run. 'Hurry up, Waleed, they're going to get away,' shouts Elyas from the other side of the river.

Waleed decides to swim to the other side. He's just going to jump into the water to cross the river, when he sees crocodiles. He's very frightened now.

'Oh no, crocodiles – how strange!' thinks Waleed for a moment. 'Crocodiles live in Africa, not here!'

Waleed's trapped with the bridge too far behind him and crocodiles in front of him! Oh no! He can't get to the bridge. He can't swim across the river. What can he do? Then he sees a rope hanging from a tree. Can he swing across?

★ ★ ★

'Waleed, wake up! You're shouting in your sleep … something about crocodiles. Are you feeling OK?' asks his mother, coming into the room.

'Oh, Mum. Yes, I'm feeling much better now!' says Waleed.

'Come on. Switch off the television. It's time to eat,' says his mum.

2 **In pairs, talk about the questions.**

1 Which real-life facts were in Waleed's dream?

2 What do you think of Elyas's actions in the story? What would you have done?

3 How do you think Waleed feels when he sees the crocodiles? What does he do to help himself?

1 Look at the pictures. What do you think they show?

2 🎧 2.07 Listen and read the text. Check your answers to Activity 1.

What was life like in the 1700s?

Many poor people didn't eat very well and so when they were ill, they could die. Lots of families had one toilet in the garden and it wasn't very clean. They also didn't have soap (and sometimes no water) to wash their hands. Doctors didn't know very much about what different illnesses were and they didn't have medicines to give people. Children also didn't have vaccinations to prevent them from getting ill and so they got illnesses like measles, chicken pox and flu.

How is life different now?

Doctors have learned a lot about preventing illnesses since the 1940s. We are told to eat a balanced diet and we also know that it's important to wash our hands before we eat or if you cut yourself. Before the 1940s, if you cut your finger, bacteria could get into the cut and so lots of people died from a disease called tetanus. Now we have vaccinations at the doctor. This is an injection to stop us getting the disease. Vaccinations contain a small amount of a virus or bacteria that help the body to fight the disease.

Sir Alexander Fleming (1881–1955): In 1928, Sir Alexander Fleming discovered penicillin and this helped to develop a group of medicines called antibiotics.

During World War I, he saw lots of soldiers die from infected cuts.

I'm going to the lab.

He started growing germs in dishes to study them.

In 1928, he noticed mould was growing in his dishes and killing the germs.

This was penicillin and it has saved the lives of millions of people.

3 Read the text again and say *yes* or *no*.

1 Some people didn't have water in the past.
2 Children had injections to stop them getting ill in the past.
3 In 1928, you could die if you cut your finger.
4 A vaccination gives you a disease.
5 Alexander Fleming died in World War I.
6 He wasn't trying to grow mould.

4 In pairs, talk about the best treatment for the problems in the box.

a nosebleed   a cold   a headache   a cut knee

1 **Read the words.** What are the differences in meaning?

study / studio / studied   doctor / medicine / bandage   who / when / where

and / but / because   century / years / months   open / opened / opening

2 **Which words in Activity 1 do you use to talk about …**

- a period of 100 years?
- a question word about a person?
- a person who tells you what medicine to take when you are ill?

3 **Complete the sentences with the words from Activity 1.**

1 Why did Jim cut his arm? _____ he fell off his bike yesterday.

2 _____ was Fred having a rest? In his bedroom.

3 Last week, we _____ the heart and brain in biology.

4 Her teacher put a _____ around her leg and then she felt better.

5 Hadi started rugby lessons in February and he broke his finger two _____ later in April.

6 I'd like to _____ a hospital for sick animals.

4 **Read the text.** What is it about?

Elizabeth Blackwell

Elizabeth was born in the south-west of England but in 1831, she moved to New York with her family. She started to work as a teacher there. She really wanted to **(1)** _____ medicine so she found some books in a library and read those.

(2) _____ she finally went to study medicine, some men in her college didn't believe that she wanted to study. In 1849, she became the first woman in America to pass all the exams she needed to be a **(3)** _____.

In 1868, she **(4)** _____ a college just for women. A year later, she went back to England to teach medicine to women in London. Today, you can read a book about her life **(5)** _____ how she helped many women become doctors in the nineteenth **(6)** _____.

> **EXAM TIP!** Read the text **once** to understand what it's about. Read it **again** to choose the best answer. Then, read it **again** to check your answers.

5 **Look at some answers to Activity 4.** Are any of the answers wrong? Why/Why not?

1 **A** study   (**B**) studied   **C** studio

2 **A** Who   (**B**) When   **C** Where

3 **A** doctor   **B** medicine   (**C**) bandage

4 **A** open   **B** opened   (**C**) opening

5 (**A**) but   **B** because   **C** and

6 **A** century   **B** months   (**C**) years

1 🎧 2.08 **Listen. Who's talking?**

1   <u>two friends</u>
2   _____
3   _____
4   _____
5   _____
6   _____

2 🎧 2.09 **Read the instructions and the options A, B and C. What do you think the question is? Listen and check.**

> You hear a student talking about a film she watched on TV. What …?
>
> **A**   an operation
> **B**   a king
> **(C)**   a queen

3 🎧 2.10 **Listen again. Is the answer correct?**

4 **Read the questions.** What are the key words?

1   Who did the girl watch the film with?
  A   her mum   **B**   her mum and her cousin
2   The film about a queen was …
  A   a history film.   **B**   a cartoon.
3   Which film did the girl want to see?
  A   the film about an operation   **B**   a film about a king
4   Which film did they watch?
  A   the cartoon   **B**   the history film

> **EXAM TIP!** Read the question and options **carefully** before you listen. Think about the situation the person is in and **circle** any **key words**. Then, think about similar words you might hear.

5 🎧 2.11 📝 **Look again at the questions in Activity 4. Listen and choose the correct answer.**

6 🎧 2.12 **Listen and choose the correct answer.**

1   What did the woman buy for her grandson?

A   a wallet   **B**   a football   **C**   a scooter

1 Choose the correct answer.

1 How long have you felt ill for?

   A Since the accident.   **B** For the accident.

2 What's wrong?

   A I'm injuring my ankle.   **B** I've injured my ankle.

3 Is your arm broken?

   A I don't know. It's been painful since I fell off my bike.

   B I don't know. It is painful since I fell off my bike.

4 How long have you had that cut?

   A Three days ago.   **B** For three days.

5 How long have you been a patient here?

   A Last Tuesday.   **B** Since last Tuesday.

2 ★ Read the diary entry. Choose the correct answer.

15th August

Dear Diary,

Lizzy is feeling much better now. We're having a special day tomorrow to celebrate that she doesn't need crutches anymore. In the morning, I'm (**1**) _____ Lizzy to the mall. I might buy her an ice cream too. At 1 pm, (**2**) _____ meeting Carl and his sister, Lily. Carl is my best friend and Lily is Lizzy's best friend. Then, in the afternoon, my (**3**) _____ driving us to the hills again. We're (**4**) _____ walking but not swimming this time – we (**5**) _____ going to the see the doctor again!

1   **A** take   **B** taking   **C** took

2   **A** we're   **B** we   **C** we'll

3   **A** aunt   **B** aunt are   **C** aunt's

4   **A** go   **B** going   **C** to go

5   **A** don't   **B** not   **C** aren't

3 Choose ten words from this unit. Record the words using the steps below.

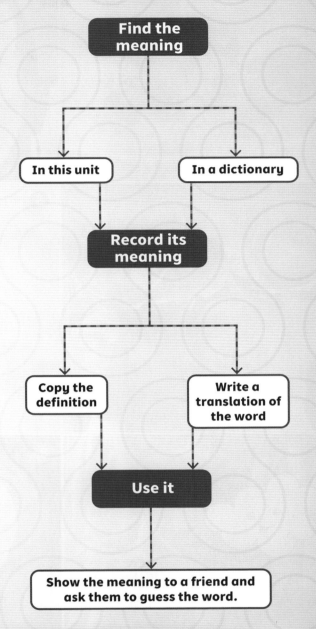

Find the meaning

In this unit   In a dictionary

Record its meaning

Copy the definition   Write a translation of the word

Use it

Show the meaning to a friend and ask them to guess the word.

Mission in action!

Present what you have found out about emergency services.

In England, if you call 999, someone will probably answer the phone in five seconds.

5 Fun foods

What food can you see? Choose three things that you'd like to eat.

Mission Take part in a cooking competition

1. Find out about food in different countries.
2. Choose a country and food. Plan how to make it.
★ Present your country and food. Choose a winner.

1 **Match the shopping lists (A–C) to the correct shopping baskets below.**
Then say the food that is in each basket.

A
Broccoli
Salmon
Chillies

B
Garlic
Lamb
Herbs
Mushrooms

C
Cabbage
Steak
Onions
Oil

2 **Listen, point and say the numbers.**   Broccoli   Number 5

3 **Draw three foods from Activity 1 and hide your pictures.** Then guess which food your partner has.

Have you got something green?   Yes, I have.

Is it a vegetable?   Yes, it is.   You've got broccoli!

4 **Play 'I went to the supermarket and bought …'.**

I went to the supermarket and bought an onion.

I went to the supermarket and bought an onion and some salmon.

I went to the supermarket and bought an onion, some salmon and ten mushrooms.

1 Look at the pictures in Activity 3. Answer the questions.

- Which food can you see in the pictures?
- What's your favourite vegetable?

2 🎧 2.14 Listen to five conversations. How many times do you hear the word 'broccoli'?

3 🎧 2.15 ⭐ Listen again. Choose the correct picture.

1  What's Claire's favourite dinner?
_____

    A   B   C

2 What would Mum like to have for dinner?
_____

    A   B   C

3  Which vegetable doesn't Emma like?
_____

    A   B   C

4  Which carrots would Karen prefer?
_____

  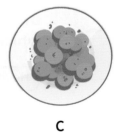

    A   B   C

5 Which food can't Tom eat?
_____

    A   B   C

EXAM TIP! Try to answer as many questions as you can the first time you listen. **Check your answers** and do any missing answers when you listen to it the second time.

4 📝 **Can you solve Claire's problem?** Think of a meal everyone at Claire's event can eat and write a menu.

⭐ Grammar look: *rather* and *prefer*

Karen: 'I prefer carrots to broccoli.'

1 What does Karen like more? **carrots / broccoli**

2 Which of the words could you add to the first sentence? **at the dinner / always**

Mum: 'I'd rather have salmon.'

3 What would Mum prefer to eat? **salmon / broccoli**

4 Which of the words can you add to Mum's answer? **at the dinner / always**

Tom: 'I'd prefer to have mushrooms.'

5 Which word is followed by the *to*-infinitive verb form (e.g. *to go, to have, to eat*)? **rather / prefer**

6 Which word is followed by the infinitive verb form without *to* (e.g. *go, have, eat*)? **rather / prefer**

We use *would rather* and *prefer* to say that we want or like one thing more than another thing.

➤ page 123

1 ⭐ **In pairs, ask and answer the questions.** Use your own ideas.

1 Do you prefer steak or salmon?

2 Do you prefer … or …?

3 For lunch tomorrow, would you prefer to … or …?

4 Do … or …?

5 …, would you …?

6 For dinner tonight, would you rather have broccoli or mushrooms?

2 **Choose one question from Activity 1 and ask your class.** Draw and write about the results.

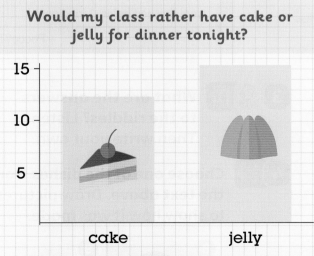

Would my class rather have cake or jelly for dinner tonight?

15 –
10 –
5 –

cake   jelly

I asked my class: 'Would you prefer cake or jelly for dinner tonight?' 12 people said they'd prefer cake. 15 people said they'd prefer jelly.

EXAM TIP! If you don't understand something, remember to use these useful phrases:

Could you repeat that, please?

Pardon?

I'm sorry, I don't understand.

⭐ **Mission Stage 1**

Find out about food in different countries.

1 **Read Jim's blog quickly.** Which ingredients do you need for each dish?

Jim's Big Blog

From **roast** chicken to **boiled** potatoes, Jenny and I love food (maybe because our dad's a chef). Last week we asked three of our dad's friends how to make some awesome dishes. Enjoy!

How was it made?!?

How was this ice cream sandwich made?

This sandwich wasn't made from bread! It was made from two cookies and some ice cream. It's an awesome dessert.

First, I got a round pot of ice cream and **cut** it into four pieces. Then I put each slice of ice cream onto a big cookie. Finally, I put another cookie on top. It was soooooooooooooo delicious!

(If you REALLY love sugar, you can melt some chocolate in a bowl over a **saucepan** and pour it onto your finished sandwich!)

– LittleLolz

How was this egg made?

Well, I think everyone knows how to **fry** an egg. You just break it and put it into a hot **frying pan** with some oil. This egg was fried like all others. But I used one little trick.

Before I put the egg in the pan, I **sliced** a large onion with a knife. Then, I took the largest ring of the onion and added it to the frying pan. Next, I put the egg into the onion ring to cook. That's how the egg was cooked in a circle. The last thing I did was make sure the egg looked happy!

– CookEggcellent

How were these caterpillars made?

Don't worry, these aren't real caterpillars! And they're very easy to make too, so they're perfect if you like healthy snacks.

To make a caterpillar, first, put six grapes on a stick and add eyes. Then, put the caterpillars in a **dish** in the freezer. I waited for about an hour (I put on the **kettle** and made myself a cup of tea) and the caterpillars were ready!

I took the caterpillars to a picnic and my friends said they were delicious. In fact, they were so popular that they were finished before I tried one!

– Pocco911

2 **Match the pictures to the words in bold in the blog.** Number 1 is 'slice'.

3 🎧 2.16 📝 **What are the answers to the riddles?** Listen. Then write your own.

4 📝 **Choose one of the dishes from the text above.** Draw pictures to show how it was made.

★ Grammar look: the passive (past simple)

'This sandwich wasn't made from bread. It was made from two cookies and some ice cream.'

1 Are the sentences active or passive? **active / passive**
2 When is the sentence talking about? **the past / the present**
3 How is the passive made (in the past simple)?
was or *wasn't* + **past participle** (e.g. *made, written, had*) /
was or *wasn't* + **infinitive** (e.g. *to make, to write, to have*)

We use the passive when we don't know who does something or when it isn't important who does it.

page 123

1 🎧 2.17 **PRONUNCIATION Listen and repeat.** page 119

2 📝 **How were the chocolate dishes made?** Write a sentence for each picture (1–8).

1
Some chocolate

melt

in a bowl over a saucepan

2
Chocolate circles

make

on a tray

3
Some balloons

fill

with air

4
The balloons

dip

into chocolate

5
The balloons

put

on the chocolate circles

6
The balloons

leave

until they were hard

7
Holes

made

in the balloons

8
The chocolate dishes

fill

with fruit

3 **Cover the sentences in Activity 2. Try to remember each one.**

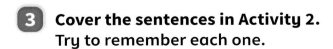
Some chocolate was melted in a bowl!

★ Mission Stage 2

Choose a country and food. Plan how to make it.

Pizza * Cheese * Tomato * Olive

1 **Have you read any diaries? What did you think of them? Do you write, or would you like to write, a diary of your own?**

The very, very interesting diary of Juana Sánchez

Monday

My parents think the show is brilliant. It's the only thing they talk about. 'Oh, Juana,' Mum said at breakfast. 'Your brother's got 63,000 subscribers to his channel!' 'Oh, Juana,' Dad said at dinner. 'Your brother's going to be world famous.' 'My last video was watched 1,000,000 times, Juana,' Carlos said. 'Have you seen the show yet?' 'No, I haven't. I'd rather clean Grandad's shoes with an old toothbrush.' I didn't really mean it, but I didn't want Carlos to get a big head.

The show's on YouTube. It's the only thing he talks about. 'Oh, Juana,' he said after dinner when I was washing up his dirty plate. 'I made chilli today. My fans loved it!'

Wednesday

Before dinner, I asked Carlos to help me lay the table. 'Well, Juana,' he said, 'I'm an internet star now, you know, and I haven't got time to lay the table. I've got my next show to think about.'

Friday

I was tired after school and wanted to relax on the sofa, but Carlos kept talking about his next show. 'On Sunday morning, I'm going to do my new recipe for spaghetti bolognese. All I need is ….' The only way I could get him to stop talking was to say, 'Carlos, on Sunday, I'm going to watch your show.'

Saturday

I had to help Dad in the garden this morning. There were worms everywhere – long, thin worms. Some people think it's strange but I love worms. So, I put some in a jar with some earth and some lettuce for them to eat.

Sunday

Carlos was like an excited child today. 'I'm so happy you're going to watch my show,' he said. 'I've got everything ready – the onions, the garlic, the herbs, the spaghetti. Now, time for my shower.' Carlos always has a shower before his shows. 'I must look my best for my fans!' he says. When he was in the bathroom, I checked on the worms. They seemed happy and had eaten all the lettuce, so I took the jar into the kitchen and found some more lettuce for them.

'Right, let's go!' said Carlos when he came back into the kitchen. 'Mum and Dad usually turn the camera on for me, Juana, but you can do it today. Are you ready? Let me get in position. OK. Press the button … now. Good morning, friends!. Today I'm going to show you how to make spaghetti bolognese. After pouring in the ingredients, I'm going to mix the … worms! Arghhhhhhhhhhhhh!'

I promise it was an accident. I left the jar of worms in the kitchen next to the spaghetti and Carlos was so excited to start filming, I forgot to move it. I did him a favour really – more people have watched this video than any of his other ones! And I'm sure he'll talk to me again – one day.

2 **In pairs, role play a conversation. Imagine you are Juana and Carlos.**

STUDENT A You are Carlos. You are very angry with Juana. You think Juana played a trick on you on purpose.

STUDENT B You are Juana. You want to say sorry to Carlos. You think it was funny but you never wanted to ruin his show and you want him to know that it was an accident.

> I'm very angry with you, Juana. My show is very important to me. Why did you let me put worms in my pot?

> I'm very sorry, Carlos. It was an accident. But at least you have more viewers now.

Social and emotional skill: apologising and showing empathy   61

1 **Read the text and look at the photos. What food groups do the foods belong to? Which nutrients do they give us? Use the words in the boxes.**

Food groups

grains, cereals and potatoes
meat, fish, nuts and beans   dairy
fruits and vegetables   fats and oils

Nutrients

calcium   vitamins and minerals
fats   proteins   carbohydrates

Superfoods?

It's important to eat a balanced diet and different foods give us different nutrients. Proteins make our muscles strong. Calcium is good for our teeth and bones and carbohydrates give us energy to exercise and play in the day.

Some foods have more nutrients than others but does this make them superfoods? Most doctors think that we shouldn't call them 'superfoods' but 'super diets' – this means we should eat a healthy, balanced diet with lots of fruit, vegetables and wholegrain foods.

Here are some foods that aren't super, but have lots of vitamins that are very good for you:

Blueberries have got vitamins K and C in them as well as other nutrients. Some people think that blueberries can protect us from heart problems and improve our memory. Try adding them to your breakfast cereal or have them for a snack.

Blueberries

Oily fish like salmon or sardines have got vitamin D, protein and some B vitamins. Oily fish has also got good fat in it. If you eat oily fish two or more times a week, it keeps your eyes and your bones healthy.

Oily fish

Broccoli has got lots of vitamins, calcium and fibre in it! It's a vegetable that you can eat in salads, soups and with meat and fish.

Broccoli

Some people think that dark chocolate is good for us, but like any food, you shouldn't eat lots of it. A little bit of dark chocolate is better than milk chocolate, but if you eat it too much, it's an unhealthy choice.

Chocolate

2 🎧 2.20 **Listen and read the text again.** Match the sentence halves.

1 Proteins are good for
2 Calcium is good for
3 We should eat
4 Blueberries have got
5 Oily fish
6 Broccoli
7 You shouldn't eat

A has got vitamin D in it.
B has lots of fibre in it.
C too much chocolate.
D vitamin K in them.
E a healthy balanced diet.
F your teeth and bones.
G your muscles.

3 **In pairs, talk about food you prefer. Do you eat any 'superfoods'?**

I'd rather eat cereal for breakfast than toast.

I prefer blueberries to strawberries.

1 **Read and answer the questions.**

1 What can you do on a cooking tour?   2 Would you like to go on one? Why/Why not?

2 **Read the question.** Think of some places Tim may have visited.

> You will hear Tim talking to a friend about a cooking tour with his dad. What day did he visit the places?

Where did Tim go?

The museum.

A shopping centre.

3 🎧 2.21 **Listen to the conversation.** Write two places you hear for each day.

1	Tuesday	
2	Wednesday	
3	Thursday	
4	Friday	
5	Saturday	

4 🎧 2.22 **Listen again and choose the correct answer.**

Days

1 Tuesday _____

2 Wednesday _____

3 Thursday _____

4 Friday _____

5 Saturday _____

Places

A apartment

B train station

C café

D museum

E TV studio

F town hall

G park

H farm

> **EXAM TIP!**
> Remember, sometimes you hear **two options**. Listen carefully for words that might mean that one option isn't correct. For example:
> * no
> * didn't
> * weren't

1 **Which phrases in the box are useful for starting a story?**

> One day, Finally, Dear Sally, Then, Lots of love, After that, Last week,
> Thanks for your email, Next, Because of this, In the end, Yesterday,

2 **Look at picture A and write a sentence.**
Use a phrase from the box in Activity 1.

3 **Which of the sentences is the best first line for this story? Why?**

1 One day, a man drinks an orange juice.

_____

2 Tony likes cooking. _____

3 Last week, John went to have dinner at a restaurant. _____

4 **Look at the rest of the story.** Choose a phrase and finish the sentences.

Then/Next, _____

Finally/In the end, _____

5 **Read two students' answers.** In pairs, talk about which story is better and why.

> In the second story, the people have names.

1

a man one day goes to eat in
ristorant. He's look his phone. A girl
enters. She is with woman. The girls
present is beutifull People is happy.

2

One day, John went to have dinner at Tony's
restaurant. He was waiting for someone and he
felt worried. Then, his daughter Betty arrived
with her mum. Betty opened her beautiful
present and Tony gave her a necklace. It was a
really fun evening.

EXAM TIP! Remember to write about **all three** pictures. Your story should have a beginning, a middle and an end.

1 **Choose the correct words to complete the sentences.**

1 I always **prefer** / **rather** broccoli to mushrooms.

2 At the picnic, I'd **prefer** / **rather** have sandwiches than potatoes and cabbage.

3 I'd rather **have** / **to have** onion sauce, please.

4 I'd prefer **to eat** / **eat** garlic than onion.

5 For lunch today, **I'd** / **I** prefer to have steak than salmon.

6 **We'd** / **We** always prefer food with lots of chilli in it.

2 **Complete the text.** Use the words in brackets and the past passive.

Last week, I went to a restaurant. The restaurant was very strange. The walls **(1)** _____ (decorate) with vegetables and the waiters **(2)** _____ (dress) as carrots!

First, I had broccoli soup. It **(3)** _____ (cook) with chilli and onion so it was delicious – but very spicy. Next, I had chicken with vegetables. The chicken **(4)** _____ (roast) perfectly and the vegetables were brilliant too. They **(5)** _____ (fry) with some lovely herbs. Finally, for dessert, I had an apple that **(6)** _____ (slice) so it looked like a bird!

3 **Choose ten words from this unit.** Record the words using the steps below.

Find the meaning

In this unit

In an online recipe

Record the example

Replace the word with a picture

Leave a space for your word

Use it

Challenge a friend to find the right word to complete your sentence.

⊛ Mission in action!

Present your country and food. Choose a winner!

I've made a main course that's popular in Portugal.

I can't wait to try it!

Mission Share ideas to protect the environment

What can you see in the pictures?
Which objects have been recycled?

1. Find environmentally friendly items at home.
2. Find out about how your items are environmentally friendly. Interview each other.
★ Present your ideas to protect your environment.

1 🎧 2.23 **Listen and point to the things in Ela's house.** Say the numbers.

> Above the stairs is a cool bulb.

> Number 2

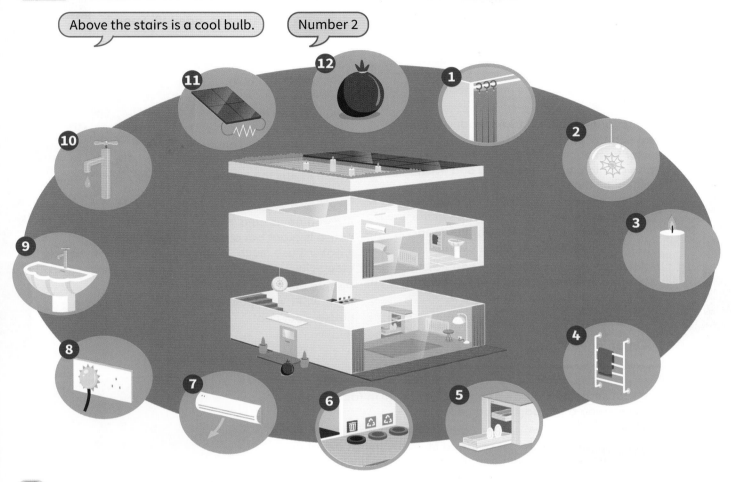

2 **In pairs, use the words in the box to check the things (1–12) in the picture.**

| curtain   dustbin   tap   electricity   rubbish   sink |
| air conditioning   dishwasher   candle   plug   bulb   heating |

> What's number 1?

> Curtain.

3 📝 **Complete the diagram with the words from Activity 2.**

4 **In pairs, share your diagrams. What are three differences?**

> I've touched a dustbin today but Walid hasn't.

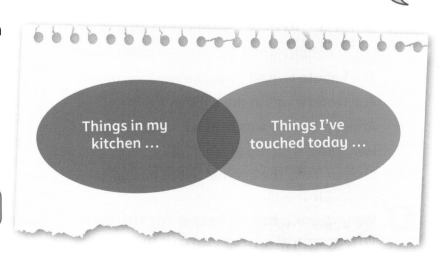

Things in my kitchen ...

Things I've touched today ...

Riku, aged 9, Japan

Ariadna, aged 10, Spain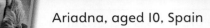

Most people aren't surprised that I don't have a dishwasher. But when I say that fish clean my dishes for me, many people don't believe me!

In my garden, there's a small room, called the kabata. In the room, there's a lot of water from our town's river. My family use the water to clean vegetables and wash dishes. A little food falls off the bowls that we wash – but that's OK because there are lots of fish living in the water, and the fish eat the food. The fish keep the water clean!

After the water comes to my kabata, it goes into the river or onto farms. A kabata is a great way to save water!

There isn't heating or air conditioning in my house.

I live in a traditional cave house – a house that's built inside a hill. The ground around the house keeps the house cool when the weather is hot, and warm when the weather is cold. My house is great because it doesn't use much electricity.

People think that I don't have Wi-Fi, electricity or even water in my cave house – but I do!

Omar, aged 11, Saudi Arabia

In my house, there isn't a dustbin. My family don't need one because we don't throw away much rubbish. In fact, we only throw away a few bags each year.

How do we do it? Well, we're careful when we go shopping – we take our own bags to put our food in. Some things are always wrapped in plastic, but we try not to buy them. Instead, we buy lots of fresh fruit and vegetables.

Finally, when we have a little rubbish, we try to use it. I've made a lot of cool things from plastic bottles!

1 **Read the article for 60 seconds. Which item *doesn't* each child have in their house?**

2 **Read the article again and say *yes* or *no*.**

1 Riku's kabata is in the kitchen of their home.

2 The kabata is used to do the washing up.

3 The water that's in the kabata is dirty.

4 Ariadna's home was built a long time ago.

5 Her house is on top of a hill.

6 She can't use the internet in her house.

7 Omar's family throw away less rubbish than most people.

8 His family don't buy things in plastic bottles, boxes or bags.

9 He often recycles things by using them in a new way.

3 **Why is each house better for the environment than normal houses? Which would you like to live in?**

> In Riku's house, they save water. It's bad for the environment to use too much water because …

⭐ **Grammar look:** *a lot of, lots of, a few, a little, many, much*

'There's a lot of water from our town's river.'
'There are lots of fish living in the water.'
'Many people don't believe me.'

'My house doesn't use much electricity.'
'When we have a little rubbish, we try to use it.'
'We only throw away a few bags each year.'

1 *Lots of* and *a lot of* / *A little* means 'a large amount of' something (e.g. money, time, food) or number of something (e.g. clothes, people, cars).

2 *Many* / *Much* means 'a large amount of' something (e.g. money, time, food). It's usually used in negative sentences and questions.

3 *Many* / *Much* means 'a large number of' something (e.g. clothes, people, cars). It's usually used in negative sentences and questions.

4 *Lots of* and *a lot of* / *A little* means 'a small amount of something' (e.g. money, time, food).

5 *A few* / *Many* means 'a small number of' something (e.g. clothes, people, cars).

page 124

1 PRONUNCIATION **Listen and repeat.** page 119

2  **Look at the three pictures and write the story. Write 35 words or more, using some of the words in the box.**

EXAM TIP! When you've finished writing, **read your text again** and check the grammar and spelling.

| a lot of | lots | a few | a little | many | much |

Did you know?

We use more than 100,000,000* bottles every day. That's the same weight as six Statues of Liberty. Many of these bottles aren't recycled and cause problems for the environment.

*one-hundred million

3 **Read your story to a small group. Whose story do you like best?**

⭐ **Mission Stage 1**

Find environmentally friendly items at home.

1 🎧 2.27 **Listen to the podcast.** Who always uses recycled paper? _____

Glenda   Alex

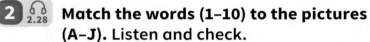

2 🎧 2.28 **Match the words (1–10) to the pictures (A–J). Listen and check.**

1	recycle	☐	6	petrol	☐
2	area	☐	7	path	☐
3	litter	☐	8	pollution	☐
4	traffic jams	☐	9	gas	☐
5	public transport	☐	10	rainforest	☐

3 🎧 2.29 **Listen again.** Which time was better for the sentences (1–6)?

		Now	When Grandma was young
1	People are better at recycling.	✓	
2	People make less rubbish.		
3	People are better at throwing away their litter.		
4	The air is cleaner.		
5	People use less gas and electricity.		
6	People save gas and electricity.		
	TOTAL:		

4 **When do you think life was better for the environment?** Discuss and vote.

⭐ Grammar look: tag questions

+   −   −   +

'Everyone recycles a lot, don't they?'   'You couldn't recycle, could you?'

'Since you started school you've travelled by car, haven't you?'

'The air was cleaner then, wasn't it?'

Tag questions change statements into questions. They're often used to check that someone agrees with us.

1 When the first part of the sentence is positive, the tag question is **positive / negative**.

2 When the first part of the sentence is negative, the tag question is **positive / negative**.

3 If the first part of the sentence has an auxiliary verb (e.g. *be, have, can* etc.), you use the **the same / a different** auxiliary verb in the tag question.

4 If the first part of the sentence doesn't have an auxiliary verb, we use *is, are* or *was* / *do, does* or *did* in the tag question.

page 124

1 **Match the sentences (1–6) to the correct tag questions (A–F).**

1 Your name's Glenda,   A wasn't it?
2 You live in London,   B isn't it?
3 Your house was built a long time ago,   C can you?
4 You don't have a dishwasher,   D have you?
5 You haven't been to the rainforest,   E don't you?
6 You can't use public transport,   F do you?

2 **Invent a character.** Ask and answer the questions from Activity 1.

Your name's Glenda, isn't it?

No, my name's Holly Wood. And I love American films!

What things in your house help the environment?

⭐ Mission Stage 2

Find out about how your items are environmentally friendly. Interview each other.

Less heating

We use lots of blankets so we don't need to put the heating on very often.

1 **Look at the pictures.** What region do you think the article is about? What can you see in the pictures?

🎧 Al-Ula in balance
2.30

The different desert habitats in the Sharaan region used to be full of plants and animals. The acacia woodlands that once covered parts of the desert have been damaged since the introduction of domestic animals like camels in the area. The animals fed, or grazed, on the plants, and now the plants have disappeared as a result.

Sharaan also used to be home to animals like the Idmi Gazelle, the Red-necked Ostrich and the endangered Arabian Leopard, but now that the acacia woodlands have shrunk, these animals have lost their habitats and are disappearing as well. The ecosystem in Sharaan is now fragile and in need of restoration so that wildlife can once again survive and thrive.

In 2019, Crown Prince Mohammed bin Salman of Saudi Arabia launched a number of ecological projects in the al-Ula desert. Among the projects is the Sharaan Nature Reserve, which aims to rebalance ecosystems in the area.

Restoring the region

The Saudi Wildlife Authority (SWA) has already planted new acacia trees. They will provide shade for other plants and the animals that have been released in the area, like the Nubian Ibex, Red-necked Ostriches, and Idmi gazelles. All of these species are under threat in the wild, but rangers are in place to help protect the area from over-grazing and from animal hunters. This is a first step in trying to rebalance the ecosystem.

Once the plant life and plant-eating species in the area recover, predators like the Arabian wolf and the Red fox will have more natural prey to hunt. Hopefully, the populations of plant and animal species will increase and the ecosystem will become balanced again.

The Arabian leopard

One predator which may be introduced is the beautiful Arabian leopard. The crown prince has started the Global Fund to raise money internationally to help protect it.

There are a number of reasons the Arabian leopard is in danger of extinction. One of the main reasons is loss of habitat, which reduces the opportunity for the leopards to find food and shelter. For this reason, the Sharaan Nature Reserve is a perfect place to reintroduce the animal.

Human beings are also a threat to the Arabian leopard. While recreational hunting is a big problem, many leopards are killed by people who think it is necessary to protect their livestock.

Rangers in the nature reserve will protect the animal from illegal hunting, and the installation of boundary fences will keep leopards and livestock apart from one another. These fences will also help to control over-grazing by livestock in specific areas and allow the acacia woodlands to regrow.

The future of Sharaan Nature Reserve

Reintroducing endangered species to the new nature reserve, and restoring natural habitat, will have a huge positive impact on the al-Ula desert region. With the help of international experts and the al-Ula community, the project will restore Sharaan's natural ecosystem. It will also bring eco-tourism to an area that is already full of archaeological treasures that include the remains of ancient cities.

The nature reserve will provide new local job opportunities, including rangers, tour guides and educators. There are even plans to build a resort in the mountains of al-Ula, to provide a comfortable base for people from all over the world who come to visit this beautiful, rebalanced desert region and its spectacular wildlife.

2 **In pairs, talk about the questions.**

1 How will the nature reserve help to restore balance to the ecosystem?
2 How will the Arabian leopard be protected in Sharaan?
3 How does the new nature reserve help the local community?

1 **Look at the pictures.** What living and non-living things can you see in them?

2 🎧 2.31 **Listen and read the text about urban ecosystems.** Find the animals – do you know them all?

Where we live

An ecosystem is all of the living and non-living things that are in an area. Living things include all of the plants and animals and non-living things are the rocks, water, soil and sand. Examples of ecosystems are an ocean, a rainforest, a pond, a desert, a river, grassland or an urban ecosystem.

As cities and towns get bigger, other ecosystems get smaller. This means that a lot of animals don't have anywhere to live and so they start to come into cities and towns to look for food and somewhere to sleep. Usually, these are small animals like mice, rats and foxes, but in some cities, there are some very unusual animals:

Leopards in Mumbai

Mumbai is a very big city and about 24 million people live there. It also has a big park called the Gandhi National Park and this is where leopards and other animals live. But as the city gets bigger, the leopards are losing their homes. So, the leopards often come into town to look for food. Some people are trying to find a different place for the leopards but the animals don't like moving to different places. So for now, people and leopards have to try and live together.

Peregrine falcons in New York

Peregrine falcons usually live near the beach but when they started to die, people in New York decided to help them live in the city. Now New York has more peregrine falcons than any other city in the world. That's amazing, isn't it? They like living in the city because there are lots of high places to make their nests where they are safe and there is a lot of food to eat too. The people of New York and the birds live happily together.

Did you know?

Birds chirp louder in cities. This is so that they can be heard by other birds – they are talking!

3 **Read the text again and in pairs, answer the questions.**

1 How have humans changed natural ecosystems?

2 Should the leopards move to a different home?

3 What problems do you think wild animals have when they live in a city?

4 What problems do you think people have when wild animals come into a city?

1 **Read the question and two answers.** Which answer is better? Why?

> Do you like these different homes?

> Yes, I do.

> No, I don't because this one is very small and this one hasn't got any curtains.

2 **Look at these pictures.** Think of one thing to say about each home.

3 **Choose an adjective and make a question.** Ask and answer the questions.

Do you think a beach house is …?

Do you think a tree house is …?

Do you think a castle is …?

Do you think a flat is …?

> fun   boring
> interesting
> expensive   noisy

> Do you think a beach house is fun?

> Yes, I do. It's fun because …

4 **Look at the pictures in Activity 3 again.** Ask and answer.

> Which of these homes do you like best? Why?

> I like the beach houses best because …

5 **Look at the questions.** Choose an answer and finish the sentences with your own ideas.

> Now, would you prefer to live in the town or the countryside? Why?

> I think … because …

> I prefer … because …

Which is more important? Living with heating or living with electricity?

> It's more important to … because …

EXAM TIP! Practise giving your opinion to a friend. Remember to use **full sentences**.

1 📝 **Read the two example exam questions below.** What does each person want to know?

Read the email from your British friend Sam.
Write an email to Sam and answer the questions.

> ○ ○ ○
>
> **From:** Sam   **To:**
>
> It's my picnic on Friday but I need some help. Can you come to my garden after school finishes at 4:30 pm? Which food can you bring? What shall we tidy up?
>
> Sam

Write 25–35 words.
Write the email on your answer sheet.

You recently joined a new afternoon club. Write a note to your English-speaking friend Linda. In your note:

- Tell her what you do at the club
- Say how much it costs
- Ask if your friend wants to go with you

Write 25–35 words.
Write the email on your answer sheet.

---

2 **Look at the answers below.** What can Costas and Federica do to improve their writing? Use the checklist.

Dear Sam,
Thanks for your message. I'm fine thanks. I know about your picnic and I can come at 4:30 on Friday. I can make and bring a very good Greek salad. I think we could tidy up the kitchen and the play area.
Bye,
Costas

Hi Emily,
I go to a nature club every Tursday after school. We make things from wood. It's fun! It's only costs 2 euros every week.
See you tomorow,
Federica

> **EXAM TIP!** To get a good mark, your writing must have **all three** things being asked for in the exam.

CHECKLIST

- [ ] Write to the person in the question.
- [ ] Write about the 3 things in the question.
- [ ] Write 25–35 words.
- [ ] Write on the answer sheet.

1 ⭐ Read the text and choose the correct words.

Last week, our art class's project was to make something using recycled materials. At first, we didn't have **(1)** _____ ideas so we did some research on the internet. Then I made a bag with **(2)** _____ old T-shirts. It's big so I can put **(3)** _____ my things in it. My friend, Anna, wanted to use **(4)** _____ old cardboard boxes. So she made a cool bookcase.

You can make amazing things with **(5)** _____ rubbish and it doesn't take **(6)** _____ time if you plan carefully and use your imagination.

1   **A** a lot of   **B** many   **C** a little
2   **A** much   **B** a little   **C** a few
3   **A** lots of   **B** much   **C** many
4   **A** many   **B** a lot of   **C** a little
5   **A** a little   **B** much   **C** a few
6   **A** many   **B** a few   **C** much

2 Say a tag question for each sentence. Then match the questions (1–6) to the answers (A–F).

1   It's hot in here, _____ ?

2   We can recycle this plastic, _____ ?

3   There isn't a dustbin here, _____ ?

4   I shouldn't leave the tap on, _____ ?

5   We're going to be late, _____ ?

6   That petrol was expensive, _____ ?

A   No, there's one outside though.

B   Yes, the air conditioning's broken.

C   Yes, we are. This traffic jam's awful!

D   Yes, it was cheaper at the other petrol station last week.

E   Yes, put it in the blue bin.

F   No, it wastes a lot of water.

3 Choose ten words from this unit. Record the words using the steps below.

Find the meaning

→ **In this unit**

→ **In a dictionary**

Record the example

→ **Draw the word**

→ **Write similar words**

Use it

→ Show the meaning of the word to a partner. Can they guess it?

 If my family and I put new bins in our house, we can recycle more plastic.

⭐ **Mission in action!**

Present your ideas to protect your environment.

Review ••• Units 4–6

1 ▶️ **Watch the video and do the quiz.**

2 **Complete the sentences using *for* or *since*.**

1 The new path has been open _____ three weeks.

2 My family have recycled everything _____ we moved to our new house.

3 This traffic jam has stopped us _____ an hour!

4 I've picked up the litter in the picnic area every day _____ a month.

5 I've been worried about the rainforest _____ I watched a TV program about it.

6 I've taken public transport to school _____ I started going there.

3 **Complete the sentences. Use the words in brackets and the present continuous.**

Next Monday, I'm not going to work. At 9 am, **(1)** _____ (**I/get up**) and boiling myself an egg for breakfast. At 10 am, **(2)** _____ (**I/drive**) to the mountains and going fishing. **(3)** _____ (**I/take**) a frying pan. If I catch a fish, I'll make a fire and fry it for my lunch. After lunch, **(4)** _____ (**I/not/answer**) the phone because I want to lie down and rest. Then, at 8 pm, I'm going to the cinema with my son. **(5)** _____ (**We/watch**) a comedy.

4 📝 **Write about your day tomorrow. Write 25–35 words.**

5 **Complete the sentences. Use the words in the box.**

> turn on   prefers (x2)   to drink   would rather (x2)

1 Ali _____ to have cream on her cake.

2 Jane _____ get blue penguin curtains than get ones with flowers.

3 My dad _____ use a dishwasher than wash up in the sink.

4 My sister _____ hotel rooms with air-conditioning.

5 Judy prefers _____ tap water to bottled water.

6 Joshua would rather _____ the air conditioning than take off his favourite jumper.

6 🎧 2.32 **Listen. Write the sentences.**

7 📝 👁 **Find the mistakes.** Write the correct sentences.

1 I spend much money on clothes.

_____

2 In my town you can go to the museum, the beach and a lot other beautiful places.

_____

3 I like it alot.

_____

4 I haven't got much DVDs.

_____

5 I don't have much things to do today.

_____

6 People spend lot of time in front of the TV.

_____

8 **Read the situations and complete the tag questions.**

1 You are at a restaurant with your family. The salmon is very expensive. What do you say?

The salmon is very expensive, isn't it?

2 You don't have enough onions for your recipe. You want to know if your friend has a spare one. What do you say?

You haven't _____

3 Your friend is coming to your house for dinner. You think she doesn't like broccoli but you want to check. What do you say?

You don't like _____

4 You think your uncle can eat mushrooms but you want to check with your mum. What do you say?

My uncle can _____

5 You think your friend goes to school by bus. What do you say?

You travel _____

9 **Choose and complete two of the challenges.**

CHALLENGE 1
Say an ingredient, cooking verb or piece of cooking equipment that starts with each of the following letters:

F-R-U-I-T S-A-L-A-D

CHALLENGE 2
Look at Unit 4. Find:
• seven things that can make you feel bad.
• three things that can make you feel better.
• a part of your body.

CHALLENGE 3
Look at the pictures of objects on pages 67 and 70. Write a list of 10 objects that you have in your home and 5 objects that you don't have.

(7) Feeling it

How would you feel in each picture? When have you felt like this?

(★) **Mission Make a 'feelings wheel'**

(1) Brainstorm different emotions you feel.

(2) Make a list of tips for feeling better.

(★) Make a feelings wheel with real suggestions.

1 **Read the poster.** Match the definitions (1–11) to the words in bold.

A I feel **relaxed** …
- when I'm at home with my cats.
- at school when I'm with my friends.

B I feel **miserable** …
- when I'm ill.
- when it rains for days and days. I like sunny weather!

C I feel **annoyed** …
- with Sam for telling Marie my secret.
- about the rain today. I want to ride my bike.

D I feel **amazed** …
- when I go to watch fireworks.
- when I see rainbows.

E I feel **positive** …
- about my team this season. (I think we'll win the league!)
- about my friends. I love you all!

F I feel **worried** …
- because I don't have a T-shirt for P.E. Can anyone lend me one?
- about going to the dentist next week.

G I feel **negative** …
- about my project – I need to try harder.
- when I can't answer a question in maths.

H I feel **satisfied** …
- when I finish some work at school and I know I've tried my best.
- after I've eaten a huge pizza!

I I feel **embarrassed** …
- when I speak in front of other people.
- when my phone rings in the library!!!!

J I feel **interested** …
- in dolphins. Did you know that some dolphins only have eight teeth but others have 250?
- in recycling old clothes. Who wants to learn sewing with me?

K I feel **bored** …
- when my friends play computer games.
- when I'm sitting in the car. But it's great to arrive at the beach or my cousin's house!

1 only thinking of the bad side of something
2 full of hope
3 free of worries
4 pleased because you have what you wanted
5 very unhappy
6 unhappy and tired because something isn't interesting
7 very surprised
8 unhappy and thinking about your problems
9 a bit angry
10 shy
11 wanting to read about, talk about or learn more about something

2 **Complete five of the *I feel* … sentences from Activity 1 so that they are true for you.**

I feel relaxed when I'm at home watching TV.

3 3.02 **PRONUNCIATION** **Listen and repeat.**

page 119

1 **Read Jim's blog quickly.** What problems do you think the people have?

Jim's Big Blog

This week we asked our friends if we could help with any of their problems. Here's what we wrote!

Helping our friends

Hello,

I love your blog! You always have interesting ideas to write about.

How can I think of ideas for my blog? I often sit in my room thinking until I feel miserable. Please help!

Thanks, Kyo_hearts

We find it hard to think of ideas for our blog too. We have to work really hard!

The best way to have a few good ideas is to have lots of ideas. You should write a long list of things you're interested in. You needn't worry if some of your ideas aren't very good and you don't have to spend more than five or ten minutes writing either. When you've finished the list you can use the best ideas in your blog.

Jim

Hi Kyo_hearts,

You ought to write about something you love. It doesn't matter if your blog's popular or not. If you're blogging about what you love, then you'll love blogging.

Jenny

Hi,

I'd like a pet to love and look after, but my parents say that I can't. I ask them but they always say I have to wait until I'm older. I'm so frustrated. Do you think I should get one without telling them?

Florenville2025

I think you ought to understand your parents. Why don't they want you to have a pet? Maybe they're worried about how much it costs? Or maybe they're annoyed with you because you often ask them about it?

You shouldn't get a pet without telling your parents. You'll be too worried about them finding it.

Jim

Hi Florenville2025,

No! NO! NO! You **MUSTN'T** get a pet without telling your parents. You should try to be satisfied with what you have. You ought to get a plant if you want something to love and look after.

If your parents say you can't have a pet, you must listen to them!

Jenny

2 ⭐ **Read the blog again.** Say which person …

1   enjoyed reading Jim and Jenny's blog.

   A   Kyo_hearts   B   Florenville2025

2   thinks it is hard to have ideas to write about.

   A   Jim   B   Jenny

3   feels a bit angry with his parents.

   A   Jenny   B   Florenville2025

4   thinks that Florenville2025 won't feel relaxed if he gets a pet.

   A   Jim   B   Jenny

> **EXAM TIP!** Make sure you know exactly which part of the text gives you the answer to the question. If it helps you, **underline the sentences** in the text which are useful.

3 **Who do you think gave the most useful advice?** What advice would you give?

★ Grammar look: *needn't, have to, should, ought to, must, mustn't*

'I have to wait until I'm older.'

'If your parents say you can't have a pet, you must listen to them!'

'You mustn't get a pet without telling your parents.'

'You needn't worry if some of your ideas aren't very good.'

'You don't have to spend more than five or ten minutes writing either.'

'You should try to be satisfied with what you have.'

'You ought to write about something you love.'

1   *Have to* and **must / should** have similar meanings. They're used when we don't choose to do something and someone else (like a parent, teacher or the police) chooses for us.

2   *Ought to / Needn't* and *don't have to* have similar meanings. They are used when we do not need to do something. Their meaning is different to *mustn't*. *Mustn't* is used when there is a rule about something you cannot do.

3   **Should** and **ought to / mustn't** have similar meanings. They are used when something is correct or a good thing to do. We can choose if we want to do these things.

page 125

1   **Read two more messages to Jim and Jenny.** Write three sentences to reply to each message. Use *needn't, have to, should, ought to, must* or *mustn't*.

1

I forgot my best friend's celebration last week and I didn't get him a card or say 'Congratulations'. I feel really miserable because of it. What should I do?

SnakeGoat

_____

_____

_____

_____

_____

_____

2

My friends want to go swimming in the river after school, but I'm worried about it. There's a big sign that says it's dangerous to swim. What should I do?

Lunchtime_Tam

2   **In pairs, share your ideas.** Which letter would you like to reply to?

I'd like to reply to Letter 1. I forgot my cousin's celebration once, so I know what SnakeGoat should do.

★ Mission **Stage 1**

Brainstorm different emotions you feel.

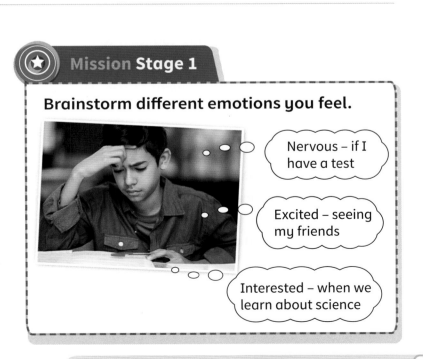

Nervous – if I have a test

Excited – seeing my friends

Interested – when we learn about science

1 **3.04** **Listen.** Where did the boy fall asleep? _____

2 **3.05** **Listen again and point to pictures 1–6.**

3 **3.06** **Complete the sentences.** Use the words in the box. Listen and check.

> breathe deeply   do exercise   go jogging
> goes to the gym   look after his health
> keep fit   reduce stress   recover   aching   diet

1 My dad said he was feeling worried because we're moving house so he wanted a way to _____ .

2 We go to the sports centre together to relax and _____ .

3 You can _____ there, like running or swimming.

4 When we _____ , we wear special glasses. It feels like we're running away from a lion!

5 While my dad _____ to lift weights, there's a big swimming pool where I go to swim with sharks.

6 After we exercise, there are lovely places to sit and _____ .

7 There's a little pool that we sit in when we've got tired, _____ legs.

8 There's a garden on the roof. You can just sit, _____ and listen to the river.

9 They've only got healthy food. A good _____ is important – so they haven't got cake or ice cream.

10 My dad always says he wants to _____ better.

4 ⭐ **In pairs, ask and answer the questions.**

1 What kinds of exercise do you like doing?

2 What do you do to look after your health?

3 What do you think are the best ways to reduce stress?

EXAM TIP! When you answer questions, use **full sentences** and try to say four things.

⭐ Grammar look: *such ... that / so ... that*

'It's so fun that my dad and I always laugh a lot!'
'It's such a relaxing place that I once fell asleep there!'

1   *So ... that* and *such ... that* are used for **surprising**, **strange or unusual / boring, uninteresting or normal** situations.

2   We use **so / such** with adjectives (e.g. *good, bad, boring*) or adverbs (e.g. *quickly, tiny*).

3   We use **so / such** with noun phrases (e.g. *an interesting person, a great cook*).

page 125

1   **Complete the sentences.** Use *so ... that* or *such ... that*.

1   I exercised for __such__ a long time __that__ my legs ached!

2   I felt _____ stressed _____ I couldn't sleep!

3   I was _____ embarrassed _____ my face was red!

4   I thought it was _____ a boring book _____ I didn't finish it!

5   I felt _____ annoyed _____ I walked away!

6   It was _____ a big sandwich _____ I couldn't eat it all!

2   **Complete the sentences with your own ideas.**

1   It was such a delicious cake that _____

2   The weather was so _____

3   The test was so difficult that _____

4   It was such a hot day that _____

3   **Work in small groups.** Talk about when three of the sentences in Activity 1 described your life.

When I went to the mountains with my grandpa, I exercised for so long that my legs ached.

When I went swimming last Monday, I swam for such a long time that my arms ached.

⭐ Mission Stage 2

Make a list of tips for feeling better. Share your list with your friend. Do they have any good ideas you missed?

How to feel better!!
☺ Play some sport
☺ Call your friend
☺ Look at photographs of your family

1 **In pairs, talk about the questions.**

1   What does a cowboy do?

2   Where do wolves live? What do they eat?

The cowboy who cried wolf

3.07

Life on the ranch was quiet. Everyone worked hard to grow plants and look after the animals, and they fell asleep straight away when night came. But one night, a noise woke them all up. AHR-WOOOOO! They knew that noise! It was a wolf, and there were a lot of calves on the ranch. Somebody would need to make sure that no wolves got into the fields.

Buck was the youngest cowboy on the ranch and he was always looking for excitement. Early the next morning, Cody, one of the older cowboys, said to Buck, 'You have to stay here today and look after the calves. There are wolves about! If you see one, you should shout, "Wolf!" The people on the ranch will come and help you.' Buck was annoyed. He wanted to ride with the others! But he had to do what Cody said. So, the cowboys rode off to the west and Buck stayed in the field to look after the calves.

Buck was so bored! He had no one to talk to, and no wolves came. Buck stared so hard that his eyes hurt. Hours passed and Buck was miserable. Finally, he had an idea. 'The ranch workers will come and talk to me if a wolf comes,' he thought. He jumped up and shouted, 'Wolf!' At once men came running from the ranch. His little sister, Blossom, came too.

'Where's the wolf?' shouted the men. 'It was over there,' said Buck. 'But it went away when I shouted.' The men waited for a few minutes, but when they didn't see a wolf, they went back to their work.

'Did you really see a wolf?' Blossom asked Buck. 'Of course I did,' he said. Blossom gave him a strange look. Buck felt embarrassed, but Blossom didn't say anything.

Text type: a story

The next day, Buck wanted to go with the other cowboys, but Cody was worried about wolves. 'You must stay and look after the calves again,' he said. So, Buck stayed! Day after day, it was the same thing, looking at a dull field of cows. By the fourth day, he was so bored and lonely that he shouted, 'Wolf!' again. Once more the men from the ranch ran to help him. They were amazed when they didn't see a wolf attacking the calves. 'Where's the wolf?' they called to Buck. 'It was over there,' said Buck. 'But it ran away when I shouted.' 'Are you sure you saw a wolf?' asked a man called Jeb. 'I definitely saw one!' said Buck. 'That's why I shouted.' The men from the ranch went away again, complaining.

Blossom was furious with her brother. 'There was NO wolf,' she said to Buck. 'You mustn't shout "wolf" again. Everybody is very annoyed with you!'

The next day, Buck suddenly heard AHR-WOOOOOO! He jumped up. It wasn't one wolf! It was 3 … 4 … 5 … a pack of wolves! 'Wolves! Wolves! Wolves!' screamed Buck. But nobody came. They didn't believe him anymore! Buck ran at the wolves, shouting. But it was too late. All the calves were dead and Buck knew he would be in BIG trouble …

2 **In pairs, talk about the questions.**

1   Who or what is responsible for the death of the calves? Why?

2   Do you ever tell lies? Why?/Why not? When might you tell a lie?

3   How do you think Buck feels when he realises he's made a mistake? Do you think he feels bad for telling lies?

1 Look at the pictures below. What different emotions can you see?

2 🎧 3.08 Listen and read the text. Why is it good to understand how other people feel?

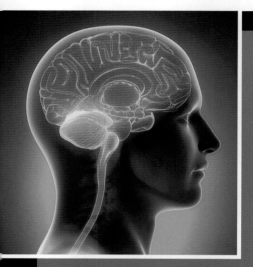

Emotional awareness

We can feel different things on different days. Sometimes we feel miserable because we had an argument with a friend and sometimes we feel worried about something. It's important to understand our feelings and learn how to show them so that we don't make our friends, our family and ourselves sad.

Babies and children show their emotions by laughing or crying because they can't say what they feel and why. As we grow up, we learn how to understand how we are feeling. This is called emotional awareness. It also helps us have good relationships with other people.

When we feel strong emotions or we are stressed, there are chemicals in our brains that can make us feel happy, annoyed or sad. This chemical is called cortisol. It can be good for us because it gives us energy. However, if we feel too stressed, then we have too much cortisol in our brains and it's difficult to sleep.

When you see your friends, you might be able to work out what they are feeling by their faces. How do you think these people feel?

It's good to think about how other people are feeling too. For example, if your friend is sad that he didn't get onto the football team and you are sad with him, you are sharing his sadness – this is called empathy. Have you ever seen that your dad is annoyed when he has to tidy your things? If you think about how your dad feels and understand that he's doing extra work and why he might feel annoyed … that's also empathy.

Empathy and emotional awareness are important for all relationships – at home, at school and at work when we are older. It helps you to understand more about the people and the world around you.

3 Read the text again and say *yes* or *no*.

1 We need to understand our own feelings before we can understand other peoples'.

2 Cortisol helps us sleep.

3 We can sometimes understand how friends feel by looking at them.

4 Adults often feel empathy when they have to tidy things.

5 You should think about how other people feel in all situations.

4 In pairs, talk about things you can do when you are feeling stressed or sad.

> When I feel stressed, I like to go outside for a walk.

> I like reading a book.

1 Look at the title and the picture and answer the questions.

1 Why do you think the club in this text is so amazing?

2 What could the boy's dream be?

2 Read the text and check your ideas.

1 **An amazing club!!**

2 Ben Bampton's just started a school club called 'Helping Dreams'. He became interested after reading about a company that helps schoolchildren who feel bored or worried. I told my dad, 'I'd like to do something like that too.' 'Let's call that company now!' he answered. 'That's how I learned about finding pieces of machines or clothes and inventing something new with them. I sell the new objects during the lunch break. The money I get helps kids in our area who feel alone. I now understand that if you want to help people, you should do it as a team.'

3 'You don't need to know lots of facts or be good at science in my club. You can make a new game from an old CD player, shoes or used handbags.'

4 Ben's simple idea has grown and his town thinks his club is fantastic! Ben would like to start his own business soon. He's finding ways to make his helpful ideas cost less. He plans to have 'Helping Dreams' clubs in every school, so any child who wants to build something can join the team for free.

5 Ben feels amazed because his club is so popular and says, 'It's important to talk to someone when you feel unhappy at school. You should try to have fun with friends, and my club helps with that too! Anything is possible! Look at me and my dream!'

3 Read the text again. Match the ideas (A–E) to the title and paragraphs (1–5).

A This tells me what the text is about. _1_

B A boy's interest in starting a club. ___

C The boy's future plans. ___

D The boy's advice. ___

E What you can do in the club. ___

4 Where does the writer or Ben say this? Find the sentences in the text.

● The money helps other children who live near the school.

● You don't need to get good marks if you want to be in the club.

● The boy's next project is to have his own business.

● Share your problems at school with someone.

5 Read the question and choose the correct answer.

Ben plans to …

A be more popular.

B have clubs like his in more schools.

C be healthier at school.

EXAM TIP! Practise reading texts **quickly** for **main ideas** and then **more carefully** to find **details**.

1 In groups, talk about what you do to relax before a school exam or test.

> I go to my friend's house.

> I eat a snack with my brother. He's so funny!

> I read my favourite book.

2 Read the start of the conversation and complete the instructions.

> You will hear (1) _____ talking to her friend
> (2) _____ about (3) _____ .
>
> **Sophie** Hi, Nura, what's the matter? Have you got a cold?
>
> **Nura** I'm very tired actually. I'm not sleeping enough at the moment.
>
> **Sophie** Are you worried about your science test?
>
> **Nura** Yes, I had a maths test yesterday and history today. If I don't sleep well, I won't get a good mark …

3 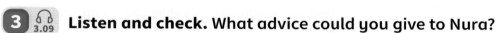 **3.09** Listen and check. What advice could you give to Nura?

4 Look at the example answer. Why is A the best answer?

Example: 0 What's wrong with Nura at the moment?

(A) She's tired.　　**B** She's got a temperature.　　**C** She's got a cold.

5 What are the questions about? Put them in the right group.

> Who feels tired at the moment?　Which test did Nura do yesterday?
> What does Nura do to stop feeling worried?　Which two things shouldn't she use late at night?
> Who believes that good sleep helps memory?　Who feels better now?

Facts	Opinions	Feelings
		Who feels tired at the moment?

6 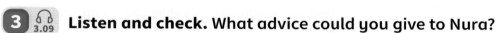 **3.10** Listen to the conversation. Answer the questions from Activity 5.

> **EXAM TIP!** Before you listen, look at the questions. Do they ask you for a fact, opinion or feeling? Think of phrases we use for these things. For example:
>
> **In fact …　I'm sure …　I'm worried …**

1 **Look at the signs and choose the correct words to complete the sentences.**

1

You **needn't** / **must** worry. It's OK to drink this water.

2

You **don't have to** / **shouldn't** swim here. It's dangerous!

3

You **should** / **mustn't** walk here. You oughtn't to run.

4

CAUTION

This sign has sharp edges.

You **have to** / **mustn't** touch this sign. You might cut yourself.

5

You **must** / **needn't** turn off your phone here. People are studying.

6

You **shouldn't** / **have to** put food in this bin. It's only for paper.

2 **Write one sentence using *so … that* or *such … that*.**

1 I felt bored during the film. I fell asleep.
   I felt so bored during the film that I fell asleep.

2 I think it's a fun gym. I go after school every day.
   _____

3 She does exercise carefully. She never gets injured.
   _____

4 I think painting is fun. I tell all my friends to try it.
   _____

5 I had a bad headache. I couldn't stand up.
   _____

6 I played football for a long time. I had to lie down to recover.
   _____

3 **Choose ten words from this unit. Record the words using the steps below.**

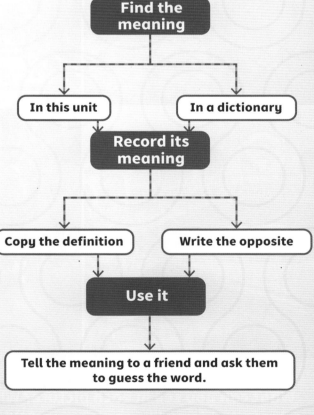

Mission in action!

Make a feelings wheel with real suggestions.

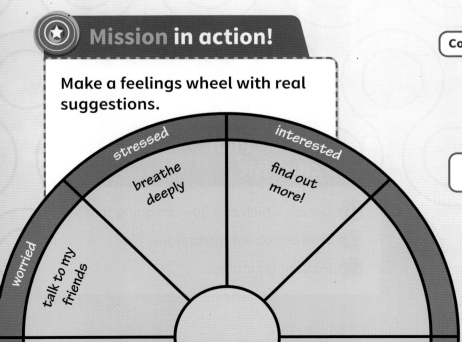

8 Pretty cities

What can you see in each picture? Which place would you like to visit most? Why?

⭐ Mission Plan a city visit

1. Decide which city you are going to visit.
2. Find out about attractions.
⭐ Present your ideas.

1 🎧 3.11 **Look at the adverts for city tours.** Match the pictures (1–10) to the words in bold in the advert. Then listen and check.

Boat tour of Jeddah

Only 80 riyal!

- See the city from the water on our one-hour **cruise**.
- Learn about Jeddah's history and see the Jeddah **tower** project.
- Take photos of some of Jeddah's most famous buildings and **monuments**.

London sports tour

- Take a **sightseeing** bus tour of London's most famous sports stadiums.
- Look round the Wimbledon Lawn Tennis museum and it's amazing **collection** of tennis prizes.
- The tour goes past Buckingham **Palace** and finishes at London's famous sports **department store**.

Call for more information

Art tour of New York

- Visit a **gallery** and see one of the U.S.A.'s best art collections.
- See amazing **sculptures** as we walk through New York's streets.
- The tour ends at the top of the Empire State Building, with amazing **views** across the whole city!

2 Write sentences about which places your class would like to visit.

We'd love _____ 😍

_____

We wouldn't mind 😐

_____

_____

We wouldn't like 🙁

_____

3 ⭐ **A teacher is going to take some students on one of the tours.** In pairs, talk about the tours and say which the students would find most interesting.

I think her class would love to visit a gallery and look at the sculptures.

Me too! And I think they wouldn't mind going on a river cruise because they could take lots of amazing photos.

EXAM TIP! To give opinions, say what would or wouldn't be a good option and **why**.

1 **Look at the pictures and choose the correct words to complete the sentences.**

1   I think the building is probably in **London** / **New York** / **Jeddah**.

2   I think the building is probably a **department store** / **monument** / **gallery**.

3   I think the painting might be by **Da Vinci** / **Van Gogh** / **Monet**.

2 🎧 3.12 **Listen to a radio show called Charlie and Chuck's Challenge and check your answers to Activity 1.**

3 🎧 3.13 ⭐ **Listen again, and write the correct answers.**

Charlie and Chuck's Challenge

About

The gallery has around **(1)** _____ paintings.

Tickets are: **(2)** _____ for children

Has amazing pictures like Van Gogh's

(3) *The _____ Night*

Information

The phone number is **(5)** _____

EXAM TIP!
Make sure you **read the notes and question** before the recording starts. Can you think of any possible answers before you listen?

4 **In pairs, answer the questions.**

1   Is there a gallery like this where you live?

2   Would you like to go on a school trip to this gallery?

★ Grammar look: indirect questions

'How many paintings are there?'

'Do you know how many paintings there are?'

1 Indirect questions are usually **more** / **less** polite then normal questions.
2 When we use indirect questions, the word order **changes** / **stays the same**.

➤ page 126

1 🎧 3.14 **PRONUNCIATION Listen and repeat.** ➤ page 119

2 Put the words in order to make questions.

1 what I can see / please? / Could you tell me / at the museum,

2 what / Do you know / time / closes? / the museum

3 the museum / where / please? / Could you tell me / is,

4 how / tickets / please? / much / Could you tell me / are

5 the / please? / Could you tell me / museum's / phone number,

6 if / Do you know / take photos / I can / at the museum?

3 Answer the questions from Activity 2 about one of the museums below.

MADINA MUSEUM

Tickets:
Adults, 40 riyals
Children (aged 5–17), 10 riyals

What you can see:
Exhibits and videos about the history and development of Masjid an-Nabawi.

Opening times: 8 am–1 pm and 4 pm–9 pm (closed on Fridays)

Finding us:
We're on Sultana Street, Al-Madinah Al-Munawarah

Photos: You can take photos anywhere in the museum.

LONDON TRANSPORT MUSEUM

Tickets:
Adult £17.50;
Free for children (under 18)

You can see:
Old buses, trains, taxis and many other things

Opening hours:
10:00 am–6:00 pm on Monday – Thursday, Saturday and Sunday
Fridays 10:00 am–8:00 pm

Address:
Covent Garden Piazza, near the River Thames

Bring a camera because you can take photos in the museum!

★ Mission Stage 1

Decide which city you are going to visit.

I really want to go to Madina. It looks so cool!

That sounds great! Let's look for tours there.

1 **Read Jim's blog.** Do you think these places are boring or beautiful?

Jim's Big Blog

Last week, Jenny and I visited London. While Jenny took photos of the famous places in London, I took photos of things that might look boring – but that I think are amazing.

Boring or beautiful? My photos of London

Jenny said, 'Oh Jim! You're not taking a photo of that, are you?' Some people say that this is London's most beautiful roundabout! That's because of the amazing glass building in the middle of the **roundabout**. In the building is a **booking office** where you can buy tickets and a cinema with the largest screen in Britain!

Jenny said, 'That's just a car park, Jim!'

This **car park** was built in 1928 – and, with 1,000 spaces, it used to be the biggest car park in the country! It used to have two different restaurants inside too. When it was built, there was even a plan to put a golf course on the top of it. Today, the building's still a car park but sometimes events like fashion or film shows happen there.

Jenny said, 'This is the ugliest place we've been all day!' I think this station's amazing.

It opened in 1863 – that's more than 150 years ago! In fact, London had the first **underground** stations in the world. Today, the trains are electric, but they didn't use to be. They used to make the air very dirty!

Jenny said, 'Really Jim? ANOTHER photo?!'

This **signpost** made me laugh a lot. It was on a normal **pavement** in London! There are lots of interesting street names in London, like Brick Lane and Pie Corner. Can you guess what used to be made on those streets?

Jenny said, 'Can't we get a map and go?'

This is the **tourist information** centre in London. Jenny went there to get a map and find out the **opening hours** for a gallery. While Jenny was chatting and Mum was getting some money from a **cash machine**, I took this photo. I love this building because it's very new, but looks amazing next to the old buildings nearby. The building is also good for the environment – its roof collects water to use in its toilets and for its gardens.

2 **Match the definitions (A–I) to the words in bold in Jim's blog.**

A Something that you walk on, next to a road

B Somewhere that you get money

C The times that a place is open

D Somewhere people leave cars

E Something next to a road that gives you information

F A train that travels under the streets

G Somewhere where you can buy tickets

H Somewhere you can ask questions about a new city

I Somewhere roads meet and that cars drive around

3 **Look at the pictures in Jim's blog.** Which words in bold in the blog can you see? Which words can't you see?

⭐ Grammar look: *used to / didn't use to*

'They used to make the air very dirty.'

'Today, the trains are electric, but they didn't use to be.'

'Can you guess what used to be made on those streets?'

1 Did trains make the air dirty in the past?
Yes / No

2 How many times did this happen?
Often / Only once

3 Does it happen now? **Yes / No**

Used to means that things happened **(4) often / once** in the past. They **(5) still / don't** happen now. It's also used for facts that were true, but aren't now.

page 126

1 **Guess which of the facts (1–4) is false.**

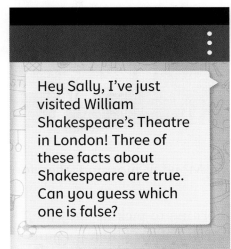

Hey Sally, I've just visited William Shakespeare's Theatre in London! Three of these facts about Shakespeare are true. Can you guess which one is false?

1 Shakespeare used to live in London.

2 Women didn't use to act in Shakespeare's plays.

3 Shakespeare used to like watching football.

4 Shakespeare's brother Edmund Shakespeare also used to write plays.

2 **Write three true sentences and one false sentence about yourself.** Use *used to* or *didn't use to*. In groups, guess the false sentences.

_____   _____

_____   _____

⭐ Mission Stage 2

Find out more about the attractions in the city.

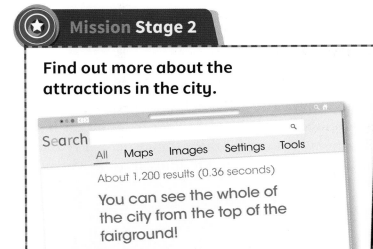

Search

All   Maps   Images   Settings   Tools

About 1,200 results (0.36 seconds)

You can see the whole of the city from the top of the fairground!

1 **What can you see in the pictures? What do you think the novel is about?**

Chapter One
The case of the missing heirloom

3.16

Chan Ming had no idea how stressful it would be to look after the family business while his father was away. There was so much to do, from new products arriving that needed to be catalogued, to attending to customers in the shop, and separating those items that were for sale from those that were in storage for safekeeping.

He had a lot of respect for his father, who always managed to stay so calm. For Chan, it was a completely new experience. He had no one to help him, and no one to ask for advice when he was unsure of something.

The phone call he received on Monday morning, therefore, sent his stress levels racing.

'I'll be there tomorrow morning to pick up the vase,' said the man on the other end of the phone. 'Thank you so much for keeping it safe for us while we were away travelling. It's such an important family heirloom. Losing it would be a tragedy.'

Chan began to sweat. His hand shook as he replaced the telephone receiver. A family heirloom. The same family heirloom his father had mentioned the last time they spoke by phone. The same family heirloom Chan had spent all weekend looking for.

The one that was missing.

He paced around the shop, frantically trying to remember the blue-and-white china vase. He searched through the pile of untidy papers on the desk – had he sold it by mistake? If so, there would surely be a receipt there somewhere. 'I really must clean this place up,' he said to himself as he worked through the mess.

No clues in the paperwork.

A bead of sweat dripped from his forehead. Outside, car horns sounded as traffic jams took over the roads leading out of the city. He checked the time on his pocket watch and realised there wasn't much of it to waste – but he needed some breathing space.

Chan quickly packed a small suitcase with enough things for a pleasant overnight trip. He looked himself over in the long mirror by the front door, then took a deep breath and headed out to his hot-air balloon, locking the shop door behind him. Some time out of the city would calm him down and prepare him for the awkward meeting he was going to have on his return. Floating above the city always relaxed him; it helped him to think straight. When he was alone, sailing across the sky, all his troubles seemed to float away too.

Not this time, though.

He recognised the man who was standing next to the balloon as he approached. 'Mr Seaton,' he said. 'This is a surprise. I wasn't expecting you until tomorrow.'

'My apologies,' replied Seaton. 'My wife is so anxious to hold our precious vase again, so I thought I'd come straight to see you.'

Chan looked nervous. 'I'm afraid I have to go out for a while. Could you drop by the shop again later? I'm so sorry for the inconvenience.'

Mr Seaton attempted a smile. 'Please let me accompany you on your journey, Chan. I've always dreamed of flying in a hot-air balloon.'

2 **In pairs, role play a conversation.** Imagine you are Chan and Mr Seaton, travelling together in the hot-air balloon.

STUDENT A You are Chan. You are worried. You need to explain to Mr Seaton that his family heirloom is missing. You think he will be angry with you for losing the vase.

STUDENT B You are Mr Seaton. You are relaxed. You want to enjoy the trip in the hot-air balloon and think that business can wait until later.

> Mr Seaton, I need to tell you something. I haven't had time to look for your vase yet but …

> It's OK, Chan. We can worry about that later. Let's enjoy this spectacular view!

1 Look at the pictures and match them to the headings (1–4).

1 Don't feed the animals ☐

2 Respect local customs and traditions ☐

3 Protect the environment ☐

4 Support local communities ☐

A

B

C NO FEEDING WILDLIFE FINES APPLY

D Masjid For Ladies

2 🎧 3.17 Listen and read the text. What ideas from Activity 1 are good for Thumama?

When you visit another place, do you think about where you put your rubbish? Do you respect the wildlife? Do you learn about the people that live there and do the same things that they do? If the answer is yes to these questions, then you are an ecotourist!

The Thumama National Park in Saudi Arabia is a natural reserve north of the city of Riyadh. The large desert area is full of mountains, valleys and hills.

Thumama has become a popular tourist destination. Farmers in the area are happy to speak to tourists and show them around. Some will even let you explore the area on one of their horses or camels. People can hire tents and camp out under the stars and enjoy the natural landscape. Visitors can rock climb and have picnics among the sand dunes.

The negative side of this tourism is the rubbish that they leave behind. With the national park being so large, it is the responsibility of visitors to the area to be respectful and keep the area clean, so that they don't spoil an amazing experience for everyone else.

Did you know

There are national parks all around the world. They cover about 6% of the Earth's surface.

3 🎧 3.18 Listen and write the correct answers.

Timanfaya National Park

Location: Lanzarote, the Canary Islands, Spain

Size: (1) _____

Popular name of the park: (2) _____

Transport: (3) _____

Interesting activity: (4) _____

Type of food: (5) _____

4 Choose a holiday location in your country. Make a list of ways that people can be responsible tourists there.

1 **Read and write the words in a sentence.** What are the different meanings?

> travel   trip   tour

_____   _____

_____   _____

_____   _____

2 **Read the text below.** Can you guess the words you don't know?

A modern travel company

Cities **(1)** _____ important places and our company, City Tourism, **(2)** _____ to help visitors explore and have fun.

Choose a **(3)** _____ with us and you'll be really surprised at how many different activities there are. The people you stay **(4)** _____ teach you something new and then you go sightseeing. For example, learn about garden bees or make bright costumes for a festival. Afterwards, you can go on a tour of the colourful street art. It's our most popular activity, so book early!

Many **(5)** _____ come back every year. This year, we are going to build little houses to look **(6)** _____ the animals that live in the city. We will keep you **(7)** _____ so it doesn't matter how old you are, you'll never be bored!

3 **Read the text again.** For each question, choose the correct answer. Why are the other choices incorrect?

2	**A** wants	**B** can	**C** need
3	**A** holiday	**B** journey	**C** trips
4	**A** by	**B** with	**C** at
5	**A** passengers	**B** families	**C** visitor
6	**A** after	**B** for	**C** to
7	**A** noisy	**B** tired	**C** busy

Example:

1 **A** is   **B** isn't   **C** are

Answer: **A**   **B**   **C**

☐ ☐ ▨

EXAM TIP! Practise **reading** all kinds of short texts and guess words you don't know.

1 In pairs, talk about the types of holidays you enjoy.

> I like going to visit my family at the beach, because it's sunny. What about you?

> I prefer to go to the city. My brother and I love shopping!

2 Look at the title. Read the text quickly. What is the text about?

Our unusual holidays

We **(1)** _used_ to have boring, sightseeing holidays. My dad always wanted to go to museums! But **(2)** _____ days, my family and I travel around the world visiting strange places. Before, we used to stay in hotels, but now we normally go camping.

We decided to go to the mountains because I love **(3)** _____ photos of wild animals with my digital camera. The **(4)** _____ exciting thing is where we sleep – our tent is high on the side of the mountain! I love it, but my sister feels **(5)** _____ worried that she can't sleep.

There are lots of animals there, and it can be dangerous. If you decide to go, you **(6)** _____ hide your food so a bear doesn't look for some in your tent!

3 Read the text above. Look at the first answer. Why is it correct?

4 Look at the text below. What kinds of words are missing?

On the river in Copenhagen

I think the best way **(1)** _____ visitors to see Copenhagen is by going on a different kind of river cruise. It's not very expensive and it's even a good way to **(2)** _____ some exercise!

In December, lots of people go to the river and take a kayak to celebrate the end of **(3)** _____ year. There are lots of lights **(4)** _____ it gets very dark in the winter! Everyone gathers together and then they travel along the river. You can pass by the parks and gardens, as well **(5)** _____ the most famous monuments.

The city looks beautiful but it can get very cold, so make sure you bring a big coat! **(6)** _____ favourite part is having a delicious hot chocolate with my family afterwards.

5 Read and write the correct answer.

> **EXAM TIP!** Remember to think about the **type of word** you need in the space.

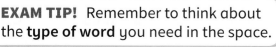

1 Choose the correct indirect questions.

1 A Do you know where Buckingham Palace is?

   B Do you know where is Buckingham Palace?

2 A Could you tell me what time does the cinema open, please?

   B Could you tell me what time the cinema opens, please?

3 A Do you remember how much were the cruise tickets?

   B Do you remember how much the cruise tickets were?

4 A Would you mind explaining how I can get to the National Gallery?

   B Would you mind explaining how can I get to the National Gallery?

5 A Do you know who is that?

   B Do you know who that is?

6 A Could you explain why the building is good for the environment, please?

   B Could you explain why is the building good for the environment, please?

2 Complete the sentences with *used to* and a verb.

1 Five years ago, I _____ on the underground a lot, but now I usually travel by bus.

2 I _____ a stamp collection. But I gave it to my friend last year.

3 I _____ in London. But I moved last year and now I live in a small village.

4 I usually go shopping at a department store. But I _____ shopping at the market.

5 The building in the town centre _____ a palace, but now it's a gallery.

6 The tourist information centre _____ at 9:30. But these days it opens at 11:00.

3 Choose ten words from this unit. Record the words using the steps below.

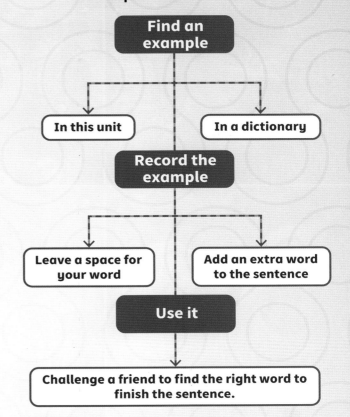

Find an example

→ **In this unit**

→ **In a dictionary**

Record the example

→ **Leave a space for your word**

→ **Add an extra word to the sentence**

Use it

→ **Challenge a friend to find the right word to finish the sentence.**

The city I chose was …

A trip to Paris!

⭐ Mission in action!

Present ideas about the city you chose and what you can do there.

9 Lights, camera, action!

What do the the pictures have to do with entertainment? Which things are familiar to you?

Mission Make a scene for a film or TV show

1. Make a mind map.
2. Plan a storyboard.
★ Present your scene. Choose the best ones!

1 **Look at the TV guide.** Match the words in the box to the pictures (1–9).

> the news   a cartoon   a chat show   a comedy   a drama
> a horror film   a documentary   an action film   a quiz show

What's picture number 1?   It's an action film.

This week on TV …

| Popular now | **Recommended for you** | Watch it again |

1 Evil men have taken Doug's cat – but he'll do anything to get it back.

2 Nemo is lost and his dad goes on a long journey to find him.

3 Interviews with top stars.

4 Join us for more lunchtime laughs!

5 Learn about the life of turtles near the beaches of Mexico.

6 Jake tells his dad the truth about the broken table.

7 The latest stories from around the world.

8 Lost. Scared. Alone. And there's something terrible in the forest …

9 We ask families what they know. Let's find out!

2 3.19 **Listen and check.**

3 3.20 **PRONUNCIATION Listen and repeat.** page 119

Language presentation 1

PHOTOS   BLOG   LINKS   CHATS

A

Question from:

Eiffel_64

Hey guys,

You're all coming to my film night next week, aren't you? I'm really excited about it. My dad's having a pizza delivered for us and we're going to watch a detective film. But I want to ask you something. Can you all let me know your favourite films? I know you all like different kinds, so I think it would be great if we chose a selection and watched them together. I want everyone to enjoy the event. I think you'll like the film I've chosen. It's about a boy who solves a mystery that no one else can!

B

CatBoy_22

Hey Eiffel_64. I'd love to go to your film night. You know what my favourite kind of films are, don't you? I love comedies. I don't mind detective films either and I like Sherlock Holmes. But watching comedies makes me feel happy. They help me to relax and forget about schoolwork for a couple of hours (but only after I've finished my homework, of course, haha!). I'd love it if we could watch a comedy film too!

C

FriendlyJ

Hey, that's such a great idea. I love animated films because I'm really interested in art and I think animators are really clever. I can choose one and take it to your film night if that's OK with everyone. But I know we won't have time to watch everybody's film choices, so I'm happy to watch a comedy and the detective film too. Let me know!

D

Sharky_McMarky

Can I bring a documentary? I know you might think that sounds boring but there's a really good one about penguins. It's my favourite and it's only half an hour long. The photography is amazing – I'm sure you'll all enjoy it. Did you know that when penguins lay eggs, the father penguins look after them while the mothers are looking for food? When the eggs become baby penguins, they have to wait a long time for their mothers to feed them. Will there be lots of pizza at your film night?

1 **Read the posts quickly.** What kind of film will each person take to the film night? Match the posts (A–D) to pictures (1–4).

2 **Read Eiffel_64's post again.** Say *yes* or *no*.

1 Eiffel_64's event is next Monday. **No!**

2 Eiffel_64 will watch a detective film at the event.

3 Eiffel_64 thinks his friends should all bring food to the event.

4 The film Eiffel_64 wants to watch is about a child detective.

3 **Write two yes/no sentences about one of the posts.** In pairs, say your sentences.

Catboy_22 wants to watch a documentary about penguins.

No, he wants to watch a comedy.

⭐ **Grammar look:** causative *have/get*

'My dad's having a pizza delivered for us.'

1 Will Eiffel_64's dad deliver the pizza himself? **Yes** / **No**

2 Who will deliver the pizza? **someone at a pizza restaurant** / **the boy**

3 We use *have* when we have asked someone to do something for us. We **do** / **don't** do it ourselves. In informal situations, we can use *get* instead of *have*.

page 126

1 🎧 3.22 **Read and match the script ideas (1–4) to A–D.** Listen and check.

1 Sarah moves to a dark, old house a long way from the town. One day, she …

A his hair dyed pink. Lots of people start visiting the mountain to see him and take his photo. He's the most famous animal on the hill …

2 A grey goat lives on a mountain and feels very lonely. But one day, he gets …

B a cool cake made, their faces painted and lots of pizzas delivered. But when the celebration started, there was one problem they hadn't thought of …

3 A farmer lives in a quiet village in a little old spaceship. One day, he has his …

C goes for a walk outside and sees a scary-looking man in the forest.

4 Two brothers were organising a celebration. They had …

D lights fixed by a strange old woman. 'Your lights turn on and off now, but don't press that big red button,' she warns.

2 **Choose one script idea from Activity 1 and finish it.**

At first, the goat loves seeing so many people. But the cars coming to see him are noisy, and some people leave litter on the hill.

⭐ **Mission Stage 1**

Make a mind map for a three minute scene.

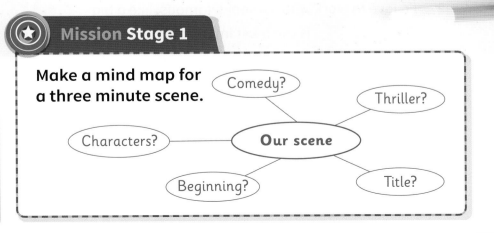

Comedy? Thriller? Characters? **Our scene** Beginning? Title?

1 **Look at the pictures.** Listen to Mark's podcast. Which idea is not in the pictures?

2 **Listen again.** Put the pictures in the order that you hear them.

travelling to China to film

paying famous actors

building old rooms in a studio

making advertisements for the film

spending money on special effects

making animations

3 **Complete the sentences from Mark's podcast.** Use the words in the box. Listen and check.

> adverts   actor   channel   heroine/hero   interviewing
> cartoons   programmes   review   series   scenes   studio

1   I'm _____ my classmates to ask what they would do if they had $250 million to make a film.
2   I'd love to work with someone famous, like a big _____ .
3   The _____ is the most important person in most films.
4   I'd spend the money by building lots of old rooms in a _____ .
5   I'd spend the money on _____ . It's really important that everyone knows about new films.
6   I'd love to make a TV _____ about tigers. I'd make six _____ that are each 30 minutes long.
7   That'd be great for the nature _____ .
8   So I'd have _____ in a futuristic city with holograms and flying cars.
9   I'd love to learn how to animate _____ .
10   And I can _____ all the films in my blog.

★ **Grammar look:** the second conditional

'If I had $250 million, I'd buy cameras and costumes for the actors.'

'If there was someone well-known in my film, I think it'd be really popular.'

1 Is having $250 million to make a film possible? **Yes / No**

2 Is it likely? **Yes / No**

3 Will there be someone well known in the film? **Probably / Probably not**

4 Will the film be popular? **Probably / Probably not**

5 We use the second conditional to talk about something that is **likely / not likely** to happen.

page 127

1 ★ **Complete the email with the words in the box. Write one word in each gap.**

> **EXAM TIP!** Look at the words that come **before and after** the gap.

had   what   would   if   ~~was~~

Dear Anwar,

I (1) _was_ watching TV yesterday, when I decided I'd like to make a film. It'd be a documentary about our town.

(2) _____ I was allowed, I'd film at the zoo. I love the animals there! If I (3) _____ a lot of money, I'd get an actor to be in the film. What about you? (4) _____ would you do if you had money to make a film? If you could ask any actor, who (5) _____ be in your film?

See you soon!

Simon

2 **What would you do if you had $250 million to make a film? Write four ideas. Share your ideas. Which idea do you like best?**

> If I had $250 million, I'd make my film in space.

3 **Tell a chain story.**

> If Tim had a million dollars, he'd buy a big house.

> If Tim had a big house, he'd keep lots of camels there.

> If Tim kept lots of camels, they'd eat all the flowers in his garden.

★ **Mission Stage 2**

In groups, make a storyboard for your scene.

> If I had more money, I'd move away.

1 **Read the title and look at the pictures.** What do you think the poem is about?

🎧 The great outdoors
3.26

Have you ever stopped to think about just how you spend your day?
I don't mean when you're studying; I mean when you're at play.
Do you often spend your time at home, sitting on your own?
Lost in social media or chatting on your phone?

It seems to me that nobody really plays outside
Like years ago when people used to go on long bike rides,
Or play a game of *Hide-and-seek* with friends around the town.
Nowadays it seems like there is nobody around.

My friends and I would always spend our Sundays in the park.
We'd get there in the morning and go home when it was dark.
No matter what the weather, we'd find a game to play,
And even when it rained on us, it never spoiled our day.

I know I'd do the same if I was still as young as you.

So why don't you consider doing something new?

Call up all your friends and ask them what they want to do.

I'm sure they'd answer straight away and love to hear from you.

I wouldn't bother messaging; I'd just pick up the phone.

I'd say, 'It's great to hear your voice. Are you all on your own?

Would you like some company? I'm feeling a bit bored.

Perhaps we could hang out a while – go ride on our skateboards.'

You'd also get some exercise and breathe in some fresh air.

Instead of being stuck inside, completely unaware

Of all the fun that you could have that's right outside your door.

It's so much more enjoyable than lying on the floor!

Take a break, run and walk, go out and play some games

With other people your own age who like to do the same.

That screen will make your eyes hurt and you'll end up ill in bed,

If you really want to stay indoors, read a book instead.

2 **In pairs, talk about the questions.**

1 Does the poet think that children had more fun in the past than they do now?

2 Why isn't it a good idea to spend all your time on your own indoors?

3 How much time do you spend online?

4 What do you like to do in your free time?

1 **Look at the pictures.** How do you think they are relevant to films?

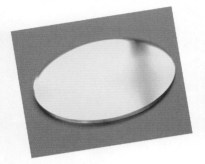

2 🎧 3.27 **Listen and read the text.** How were special effects different in the past?

Special effects in film

Have you ever watched a film and thought, 'How did the spacecraft fly?' or 'How did they film that action on a burning ship?' Film makers make these scenes by using special effects. These are artificial images that look like they are real but are created by artists and technical experts.

Quite often, the action is filmed on a green screen and then special effects are added on a computer. Sometimes the effects are so good that the experts win awards for their work.

Special effects in the past

Before the use of CGI (computer generated images) in cinema, it was difficult to make exciting special effects that looked real. Special effects artists used optical illusions and visual effects like painted sets, complicated make-up or models.

The *Star Wars* films have amazing special effects, but the original film, which was made in 1977, used miniature models of spaceships, made from wood. The film makers also used mirrors to make the main character's 'landspeeder' look like it was floating above the ground.

Make your own special effects

You can make your own special effects using your mobile phone or objects at home. Try putting a pencil into a clear glass full of water and then look at the pencil through the glass – how does it look? There are lots of apps that you can use which put special effects on photos – you can be an animal or take photos and change the way they look. We can even have videos changed on our phones – why not try it?

3 **Read the text again and answer the questions.**

1 What does CGI mean?
2 When was the first *Star Wars* film made?
3 What did they use to make the landspeeder look like it was floating?
4 What effects can we use on our phones?

4 **You are a film maker and you haven't got a computer.** In pairs, talk about how to make the scenes below.

- a landing on the moon
- a trip under the sea
- a snow storm

1 **Look and read.** Do you need all of these things to tell a story? Which do you think is the most important?

characters   action   a place   a time   names

2 **Look at picture A and answer the questions.**

A

1   Who are the characters? What are their names?
_____

2   Where are they? _____

3   What are they doing? _____

3 **Read the beginning of the story.** What things in picture A does this student write about?

> Last night, Oliver and his brother went to the cinema..........
> Oliver bought some snacks while Peter bought the tickets....

4 **Look at picture B and read the middle of the story.** Which type of film does the student write about?

B

... the tickets. They sat down and the action film started............

5 **Look at picture C. What happened?** Tell your partner. Use the words in the box or your own words.

a brave hero   special effects   was scared
funny   laughed   pointed

C

6 **Write about the end of the story.**

> Peter was scared! ....
_____
_____

7 **Swap stories.** Give your friend's story a mark. 1 is poor and 5 is excellent. Write three things they can do to improve.

EXAM TIP! Try to write between 35 and 45 words. You will **lose marks** if you write less than 35 words.

1 **Read the question and Katerina's reply.** What has Tanya forgotten to include in her email? _____

You must answer this question. Write your answer in about 100 words.
Read this message from your English-speaking friend Tanya and the notes you have made.

Describe the best one. ——

Yes – ask what time. ——

Suggest … ——

> TO:
> FROM: Tanya
>
> Hello!
>
> What programmes or films have you watched on TV this week?
>
> I saw the first episode of the new chat show on Friday. It was on the kids' channel and it got some great reviews. Would you like to come with me to the TV studio on Saturday?
>
> Dad says he can give you a lift or you and your mum can meet us there. Which do you prefer?
>
> What shall we do after the show? It finishes at 8 pm.

—— **Tell Tanya**

Write your email to Tanya, using all the notes.

Hi Tanya,

I watched a cool documentary about modern heroes and heroines. It was incredible! But it finished at midnight so I was really tired the next day at school.

I'd love to come with you to the studio. I'm free all day on Saturday. What time do they start filming the show?

I'm happy to get a lift with you and your dad. My mum also says we can get the underground so we can meet you at the studio. Why don't we go out for something to eat after the show? We both like that new Mexican restaurant.

Write soon, Katerina

2 **Which sentences in the reply from Katerina answer the notes on the email?**

_____

_____

_____

3 **Add at least one other way to start and finish an email.**

Start	Finish	Sign your name
Hi Tanya,	Write soon,	Katerina

> **EXAM TIP!** You should always put **your name** at the end of an email.

1 Complete the text. Use the words in the box.

> had/got x3   built   cut   painted

My favourite actor moved into a castle a few weeks ago – the castle was very old so she **(1)** _____ a lot of things changed. She had all of the walls in her house **(2)** _____ gold and she **(3)** _____ thick red carpets put on all the floors. In the garden, she had a golf course and swimming pool **(4)** _____ – and she **(5)** _____ some of the plants **(6)** _____ to look like elephants!

2 Complete the sentences.

1 I read the review so I didn't watch the film.

If I _hadn't read_ the review, I would have _watched_ the film.

2 I didn't see my favourite actor at the shops so I didn't have a photo taken with him.

If I _____ my favourite actor at the shops, I would have _____ a photo taken with him.

3 I saw the interview, so I know that the actor has 20 cats.

If I hadn't _____ , I wouldn't have _____ .

4 The hero lost his phone, so he didn't call the president.

If _____

5 I saw the advert, so I bought a new computer.

_____

3 Choose ten words from this unit. Record the words using the steps below.

```
Build your words
        ↓
Choose 10 words from this unit
        ↓
Look it up
   ↓      ↓      ↓
In a dictionary   Online   In this book
        ↓
Practise
   ↓             ↓
Write the definition   Write similar words
        ↓
Show
   ↓             ↓
Write in a sentence   Say it to a friend
```

This comedy is going to be so funny!

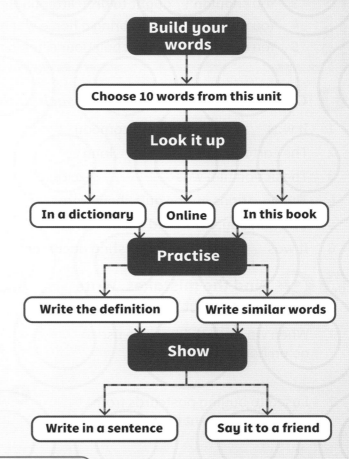

Mission in action!

- Present your scene.
- Watch and make notes.
- Vote for the best scenes!

Review ••• Units 7–9

1 ▶ **Watch the video and do the quiz.**

2 **Choose the correct words to complete the sentences.**

Tips for visiting our town

1 You **should** / **mustn't** ask about the opening hours at the tourist information centre.
2 You **mustn't** / **have to** have a picnic on the roundabout.
3 You **shouldn't** / **ought to** drop litter on the pavement.
4 You **mustn't** / **have to** bring a horse when you take the underground.
5 You **ought to** / **mustn't** buy your cinema tickets at the booking office.

3 **Complete the sentences.** Use *such … that / so … that*.

1 It was _____ a funny comedy _____ I woke my cat up because I laughed so loudly.
2 The cartoon was _____ long _____ I fell asleep before it finished.
3 The action film was _____ exciting _____ I told my friends to see it too.
4 The questions on the quiz show were _____ easy _____ I only got one wrong.
5 On Thursday, I watched a film. It was _____ a terrifying horror film _____ I couldn't sleep.
6 It was _____ an interesting documentary _____ I watched it twice.

4 👁 **Find the mistakes. Write the correct sentences.**

1 When we were children, we use to go on holiday together.
_____

2 I used to buying postcards from every place I went to on holiday.
_____

3 In the past, people were poor and they used to living in small houses.
_____

4 The cinema is in town where we use to go every weekend.
_____

5 I used to cycling in the countryside every day.
_____

5 **A health expert is coming to your school. Say the questions as indirect questions.**

> Please could you tell me … ?   Do you know … ?
> Would you mind explaining … ?

1 Why is diet important for a healthy life?

2 How often do I need to go jogging to be healthy?

3 How can I reduce stress?

4 How much exercise do I need to do each week?

5 What should I do to recover after I've exercised?

6 How do you like to keep fit?

6 In pairs, talk about what the town has had done.

> They've had the buildings cleaned.

7 Complete the texts.

A

(1) _____ I found $250 million, I'd be amazed. First, I'd go shopping, then I'd get some presents for my family. I think my dad (2) _____ like a helicopter!

B

If my rabbit could talk, I'd like to know what its favourite foods are. I think he likes carrots, but perhaps he prefers cake! (1) _____ also like to know (2) _____ he likes living with me, or if he'd prefer to live in the wild.

C

If I was a fruit, (1) _____ be a coconut because I'm very relaxed. I'd love to live somewhere warm – a beach would be great too. I (2) _____ like it if people tried to eat me though!

8 Complete the sentences (A–D).

A If I was three metres tall, _____ .

B If I found $250 million behind my sofa, _____ .

C If my rabbit could talk, _____ .

D If I could live anywhere in the world, _____ .

9 Choose and complete two of the challenges.

CHALLENGE 1
Think of a feeling or emotion that starts with each of the following letters:
B-R-A-I-N M-A-P-S

CHALLENGE 2
Look at Unit 8 pages 93 and 96. What are five things that the place you live has got? What are five things that the place you live hasn't got?

CHALLENGE 3
Look at Unit 9. Find:
● three exciting kinds of TV programme.
● two funny kinds of TV programme.
● three kinds of TV programme where you learn new things.

Pronunciation

Unit 1 Plural pronunciation of 's'

3 🎧 1.04 **Listen and repeat.** Then listen again and write the words.

/z/	/s/
days	

Unit 2 Syllabus stress in two-syllable words

4 🎧 1.17 **Listen and repeat.** Then listen again and underline the stress in each word.

1 laptop
2 keyboard
3 software
4 handbag
5 raincoat

6 hardware
7 printer
8 program
9 tracksuit
10 costume

Unit 3 Contracted forms

1 🎧 1.26 **Listen and repeat.** Then listen again, which verb form do you hear?

1 shouldn't   should
2 can   can't
3 wouldn't   would

Unit 4 Sentence stress

1 🎧 2.05 **Listen and repeat.** Then listen again and underline the stressed words.

1 How long have you been ill?
2 I've been ill for a while.
3 How long have you had a fever?
4 I've had it since last week.

Unit 5 Verb endings in the past

 1 **Listen and repeat.** Then listen again and write the words in the correct column.

/id/	/t/	/d/
planted	cooked	rained

Unit 6 Schwa

 1 **Listen and repeat.** Then tick the words or phrases with unstressed syllables.

1 dishwasher
2 the dishwasher
3 The dishwasher is in the kitchen.
4 curtains
5 the curtains
6 We've had the curtains for a long time.

2 **Listen again. Underline the unstressed syllables.**

Unit 7 /b/ /v/ /w/

 3 **Listen and repeat.** Then write the words in the correct column.

/v/	/b/	/w/
positive		

Unit 8 Intonation in questions

 1 **Listen and repeat.** Which questions are pronounced politely?

Unit 9 Word stress

 3 **Listen and repeat.** Then underline the stressed syllables.

1 cartoon
2 action
3 broccoli
4 amazed
5 sightseeing
6 gallery
7 soap opera
8 embarrassed
9 onion
10 accident

⭐ Grammar look!

UNIT 1 Comparative adjectives, adverbs and *as … as*

For short adjectives ending in a vowel + a consonant, double the last letter and add -er.

big > bigg**er**

*My raincoat is **bigger than** my jeans.*

For short adjectives ending in -e, add r.

large > larg**er**

*Canada is **larger than** India.*

For two syllable adjectives ending in -y, change the y to i and add -er.

heav**y** > heav**ier**

*Elephants are **heavier** than crocodiles.*

For longer adjectives put *more/less*, in front of the adjective.

important > **more**/**less** exciting

*Swimming is **more exciting than** tennis.*

(not) as … as …

We can use *(not) as … as …* to say something is (not) the same.

*My brother is **not as tall as** me.*

*My hair is **not as long as** my sister's.*

Practice

1 **Complete the sentences.**

1 My shoes are _____ my brothers! (big)

2 Maths is _____ science. (difficult)

3 The Statue of Liberty isn't _____ _____ the Empire State Building. (tall)

4 The heart of a blue whale is _____ _____ a polar bear. (heavy)

5 This programme about dinosaurs is _____ _____ the one about penguins. (bad)

6 My pet is _____ to my bed _____ the kitchen. (close)

UNIT 1 The present simple with future meaning

We use the present simple to talk about events that are part of a future plan or timetable.

*The train **leaves** at 8 am.*

*The test **is** on Tuesday next week.*

*What time **do** you land?*

Practice

1 **Complete the sentences. Use the correct form of the words in the box.**

| be   leave   start   go |

1 Hurry up! The film _____ in ten minutes.

2 Our train _____ at 10:45 am tomorrow.

3 She _____ to Spain in June on holiday.

4 The maths test _____ next Thursday.

UNIT 2 The zero and first conditional

We use conditional sentences to talk about possible situations or actions and their results. They have two clauses: an *if*-clause and a main clause.

We use the first conditional to talk about things which we think will happen.

We use the zero conditional to talk about things which are always true.

	If clause	Main clause
First conditional:	*If we go by bus,*	*we'll get there late.*
Zero conditional:	*If my laptop doesn't work,*	*I ask my dad.*

Practice

1 📝 **Match the sentence halves.**

1 If I get home soon, …
2 If my team wins the match, …
3 If you put money in the machine, …
4 If my sister forgets her homework again, …
5 If my dad's computer goes wrong, …

a you get a chocolate bar.
b her teacher will be really angry.
c I'll have a celebration at my house!
d I'll call you.
e he sits with his head in his hands.

UNIT 3 The passive (present simple)

We form passive verbs with the correct tense of the verb *be* + past participle. We use passive verbs when we don't know who does something or when we don't need to know who did something.

To say who did something, we use the passive + *by* + the person or thing.

*Maths **is taught** in all schools.* (They teach maths in all schools.)

*Cricket **is** usually **played** in the summer.*

*Maths **is taught by** Mr Little.*

Practice

1 **Complete the sentences. Use the words in brackets and the present simple passive.**

1 A lot of tea _____ in China. (grow)
2 Millions of bottles of water_____ every day. (sell
3 Videos _____ here every night. (play)
4 Our furniture _____ out of wood. (make)
5 Thousands of phones _____ every day. (lose)
6 I _____ on Fridays. (pay)

Unit 3 Modal verbs

We use *can/can't* or *could/couldn't* + infinitive without *to* to talk about ability or inability.

To talk about the past we use *could*.

***Can** Anna speak French? No, she **can't** but she **can** speak Chinese.*

*Max **could** walk when he was one, but he **couldn't** talk until he was two.*

***Could** he talk when he was one? No, he **couldn't**.*

We use *may, might* + infinitive without *to* to talk about something when we are not sure.

*It **may** be sunny tomorrow.*

*We **might** not go to Jack's place at the weekend.*

We can use *might, may* and *could* to talk about possibilities in the present or the future. But we can only use *can* to talk about possibilities in the present.

*It **might** be very hot tomorrow.*

*We **may** go swimming this afternoon.*

*There **could** be a storm later this evening.*

*It **can** snow here in April, but it doesn't often happen.*

The form of these verbs never changes. For example, we cannot say: *He cans. / They mighted.*

We use the question forms *May I …* or *Could I …* to ask for permission, not to talk about possibilities.

We rarely use the short forms *mayn't* or *mightn't*.

We often use *would* to make requests. It's a more polite and indirect form of *will*.

***Would** you like to play golf?*

We often use *would* (or the contracted form *'d*) in the main clause of a conditional sentence when we talk about imagined situations.

*He **wouldn't** like it if you wore his helmet.*

We use *shall I* and *shall we* to make offers and suggestions, and to ask for advice.

***Shall** I get you some medicine?*

The negative form of *shall* is *shan't*. We don't use *don't, doesn't, didn't* with *shall*.

*I **shan't** be home tomorrow night.*

Practice

1 **Complete sentences with _can('t)_, _could(n't)_, _may_, _might_, _would_ or _shall_. Sometimes more than one answer is possible.**

1   I've looked everywhere for my mobile, but I _____ find it.
2   My brother _____ swim when he was less than a year old.
3   I'm not sure what to do tonight. I _____ go to Jo's house.
4   _____ I put this here?
5   Polly isn't looking very well. I think she _____ have flu.
6   I _____ play cricket really well.
7   _____ you like to come to the cinema with me?
8   Kieran _____ ride a bike until he was 12.

Unit 4   The present perfect with _how long_, _for_ and _since_.

We use the present perfect to talk about something that started in the past and continues into the present.

Use the present perfect with _for_ to talk about a period of time

I've studied English **for** six years. _We've lived in Berlin for three months._

Use the present perfect with _since_ to talk about points in time or when something began.

I've studied English **since** 2015. **We've lived** in Berlin **since** June.

We use **How long ...?** to ask about the duration of a state or activity.

A   **How long have** you **been** ill?
B   Since yesterday.

Practice

1 **Choose the correct words to complete the sentences.**

1   I haven't seen my sister for **last weekend / two weeks**.
2   My parents have been married for **1999 / 14 years**.
3   I haven't done any homework since **last weekend / two weeks**.
4   I've had my bike since **January / six months**.
5   My father has worked as a doctor for 23 **years ago / years**.
6   Juan has played tennis since **the age of nine / seven years**.

Unit 4   The present continuous for future plans

We can use the present continuous to talk about the future. It shows that we have already decided something and usually that we have already made a plan or arrangements.

I'm seeing Alice on Saturday.

_He's_ not _going_ to the match.

We're leaving in the morning.

Spelling _-ing_ forms

Most verbs: add _-ing_ to the infinitive (_watching/finding_)

Verbs ending in _-e_: take off _-e_ and add _-ing_ (_liking/writing_)

Verbs ending in one vowel and one consonant: repeat the last consonant and add _-ing_ (_putting/running_)

Practice

1 **Read the sentences and say 'future' or 'now'.**

1 We're seeing that new film tomorrow. I bought the tickets online.

2 He's going on holiday on Tuesday.

3 I'm doing this project at the moment so I can't chat.

4 She's not listening to me.

5 They're moving house next Thursday.

6 Are you watching this?

Unit 5 *Rather* and *prefer*

We use *prefer* to say we like one thing or activity more than another. We can use a prepositional phrase with *to* when we compare two things or actions.

*I **prefer** tea **to** coffee.*

*We **prefer** going by ferry **to** flying.*

We use *would prefer* or *'d prefer*, followed by the infinitive with *to* or a noun, to talk about present and future preferences.

*I**'d prefer to go** swimming.*

***Would** you **prefer chicken** or **lamb**?*

*She**'d prefer not to drive** at night.*

We use *would rather* or *'d rather* followed by the infinitive without *to*, to talk about preferring one thing to another.

*I**'d rather stay** at home tonight.*

***Would** you **rather play** rugby or football?*

Practice

1 **Use one phrase from each box to make sentences.**

I'd rather
She'd prefer
Would you prefer
I prefer
Would you rather
He prefers

stay at home tonight.
salmon to steak.
to drive or catch the train?
swimming to running.
watch a film or go for pizza?
walking to school to cycling.

Unit 5 The passive (past simple)

We form the passive by using a form of the verb *be* followed by the past participle of the main verb.

*Our school **was built** in 2012.*

We use the passive …

- when we are more interested in who or what is affected by the action.

  *My car **was made** in France.* (I am more interested in my car than workers or the company that made it.)

- if we don't know who did the action.

  *My bike **was stolen** yesterday.* (I don't know who stole it.)

- when who or what did something is obvious, so doesn't need saying.

  *The driver of the car **was arrested**.* (We know that the police arrest people so we don't need to say this.)

To say who or what did the action in a passive sentence we can add a *by* phrase (this thing or person is called the agent).

*This film **was directed by** Steven Spielberg.* (Steven Spielberg is the agent.)

Practice

1 **Complete the sentences. Use the words in the brackets and the present or past passive.**

1 Last year's final, _____ (play) in the new stadium and _____ (watch) by over two million people.

2 I _____ (give) a new watch when I passed my exams.

3 Our house _____ (build) twenty years ago.

4 Our rubbish _____ (collect) once a week. Some of it _____ (recycle) but the rest _____ (take) to a special site outside the town.

Unit 6 *a lot of, lots of, a few, a little, many, much*

These words and phrases are quantifiers. They tell us how much or how little of something there is.

For small quantities use …

- *a few* with plural countable nouns.

  A few *people in my class speak Russian.*

- *a little* with uncountable nouns.

  I'd like **a little** *advice about going to university, please.*

For large quantities use …

- *many* with plural countable nouns.

  There aren't **many** *trains at night.*

  How **many** *times have you been to London?*

- *much* with uncountable nouns in questions and negative sentences.

  How **much** *money do you need?*

  We don't have **much** *time.*

- *a lot of* or *lots of* with plural countable nouns or uncountable nouns.

  A lot/lots of *students ride bikes to college.*

  You can save **a lot/lots of** *money if you cycle or walk.*

Practice

1 **Correct the sentences.**

1 We haven't got many time. Let's hurry.

_____

2 I drink a few water as soon as I wake up.

_____

3 There are a lot things we need to discuss.

_____

4 There isn't many traffic in town.

_____

5 I've only got little money.

_____

6 How much pairs of shoes have you got?

_____

Unit 6 Tag questions

Tags are either questions, statements or imperatives added to a clause to invite a response from the listener.

Tags consist of one of the auxiliary verbs *be, do* or *have* or a modal verb, plus a subject, which is most commonly a pronoun.

When we use the auxiliaries *be, do* or *have* or a modal verb in the main clause, this verb is used in the tag.

If there is no auxiliary or modal verb in the main clause, we use *do, does, did* in the tag.

Main clause	be, do, have, modal	Subject pronoun
He plays hockey,	doesn't	he?
She's cooking dinner,	isn't	she?
You can't fix cars,	can	you?
They act well,	don't	they?
We can stay here,	can't	we?
She's been to Italy,	hasn't	she?

Practice

1 **Write the tag questions.**

1 The shops don't open until 9:30, _____ ?

2 You can ride a bike, _____ ?

3 Tony plays football well, _____ ?

4 You haven't seen Mum, _____ ?

5 She's very clever, _____ ?

6 You can't see my mobile phone, _____ ?

7 They aren't very quiet, _____ ?

Unit 7 *needn't, have to, should, ought to, must, mustn't*

needn't

We use *need* mostly in the negative form to say that there is no necessity to do something. We form the negative by adding *not* after *need*. *Need not* can be contracted to *needn't*.

*You **needn't** take off your shoes.*

have to

We use *have/has to* + infinitive to talk about things that we need to do.

*We **have to** go to school five days a week.*

We use *don't have/doesn't have to* + infinitive to talk about things that we do not need to do.

*We **don't have to** go to school at the weekend.*

should and ought to

Should and *ought to* have similar meanings and uses. *Ought to* is more formal and less common than *should*.

We use *should* to talk about what is the best thing to do in a situation. We often use *should* to give advice.

We use the infinitive without *to* with *should* but *ought* is followed by *to*.

*There **should** be four people in a team.*

*There **ought to** be four people in a team.*

*He **shouldn't shout** so loudly.*

must/mustn't

Use *must/mustn't* + infinitive without *to* …

* to talk about rules.

  *We **must be** at school by 8:30 every morning.*

* to give strong advice.

  *You **must be** careful when you cross the road.*
  *You **mustn't cross** without looking.*

Must does not change its form.

We do not use *must* in questions. We use *have to*.

*Do you **have to** wear uniform for school?*

There is no simple past form of *must*. We use *had to*.

*We **had to** be at school at 7:30 yesterday.*

Practice

1 **Complete the sentences with *need(n't), (don't) have to, should(n't), ought to* or *must(n't)*.**

1 I _____ do any homework tonight.

2 Students _____ be late to school.

3 We _____ hurry – there's lots of time.

4 You _____ to wear your coat – it's cold.

5 You _____ switch your mobile off in class.

6 I _____ practise English every day.

7 I _____ to have my hair cut.

Unit 7 *such … that/so … that*

We use *so* and *such* as intensifiers to mean 'very, very'.

*It was **so** dark **(that)** we could hardly see.*

We don't use *so* before an adjective + a noun. We use *such*.

*She took **such a lovely photo** of my cat **that** I cried.*

Not ~~She took so a lovely photo of my cat that I cried.~~

Practice

1 📝 **Match the sentence halves.**

1	It was such a …	A	that I couldn't go to the doctor.
2	It was such …	B	that I'm sure he'll do well.
3	I was so ill …	C	hot chilli that I couldn't eat it.
4	She was so embarrassed …	D	a bad storm that the tree fell down.
5	He is such a good student …	E	that she hid her face.

Unit 8 Indirect questions

Indirect questions are a polite way of asking for information.

Direct questions	Indirect questions
Are you busy later?	Could you tell me if you're busy later?
Do you know the time?	I was wondering if you know the time.
Where do you work?	I'd like to know where you work.
When did we last meet?	I can't remember when we last met.

The word order in indirect questions is the same as for sentences. We do not use auxiliary verbs *do*, *does* or *did*.

If there is no question word (*what*, *when* etc.), use *if* or *whether*.

In indirect questions the tense does not change.

Practice

1 Rewrite the questions as indirect questions. Start with the phrase in brackets.

1 Where do you live? (Could you tell me …)
2 Are you doing anything at the weekend? (I was wondering …)
3 What did we do last weekend? (I can't remember …)
4 What did you think of the film? (I'd like to know …)

Unit 8 *Used to / didn't use to*

Affirmative / Negative forms

I/you/he/she/it/we/they	used to didn't use to	enjoy watching football.

Question forms

Did	I/you/he/she/it/we/they	use to	play football?

We use *used to* + the infinitive to talk about …

*   things that happened regularly in the past but don't happen now.

    I **used to drink** tea for breakfast, but now I always drink coffee.

*   actions that didn't happen in the past, but happen now.

    I **didn't use to drink** coffee, but now I have three cups a day.

*   past states or conditions that are no longer true.

    I **used to have** long dark hair.
    I **didn't use to** like carrots.

In the negative and question forms, the spelling is *use* not *used*.

Used to only refers to the past. There is no present form.

Practice

1 Rewrite the sentences. Use the correct form of *used to*.

1 I like hot weather now, but I didn't in the past.
2 My brother played football regularly until he broke his leg.
3 My hair was black once.
4 Did you go on holiday with your parents when you were a child?
5 When I was younger, I didn't get up late.

Unit 9 Causative *have/get*

We use *have something done* to talk about things we ask other people to do for us, things that we do not want to, or cannot, do ourselves.

Get something done has the same meaning but is more informal.

I'm **getting my hair cut** tomorrow.

The order of words is *have* + object + past participle. The incorrect word order changes the meaning.

*She **has** her **hair cut**.* (Someone does it for her.)

*She **has cut** her **hair**.* (She did it herself.)

We can use *have something done* in any tense.

*I (don't) **have** my hair **cut** every week.*

*We're (not) **having** our flat **decorated**.*

*We **had** (didn't have) our computer **repaired** yesterday.*

*We'll (We won't) **have** our **car washed** tomorrow.*

*We should **have** our **broken** window **mended**.*

*Have you **had** your jacket **cleaned** recently?*

Practice

1 **Put the words in order.**

1 you / your / had / cut / hair?
Have _____ *you had your hair cut?*

2 bedroom / have / painted / might / my / blue
I _____

3 fixed / had / Michael / yet? / bike / his
Has _____

4 get / teeth / every / my / months / polished / six
I _____

5 checked / your / computer / have / viruses / should / for
You _____

Unit 9 The second conditional

We use the second conditional to talk about unlikely situations/actions. We can also use it to imagine things.

If clauses can come before or after the result clause but if the *if* clause comes before the result clause, it is followed by a comma.

We can use *were* instead of *was* in second conditional *if* clauses.

If clause: If + past verb	**Result clause: would + infinitive**
If we **went** by bike,	*we'**d get** there very late.*
If I **were/was** you,	*I'**d look** for a new hobby.*

OR

*We'**d get** there very late **if** we **went** by bike.*

*I'**d look** for a new hobby **if** I **were** you.*

Practice

1 **Write second conditional sentences.**

1 I'd like to play basketball but I'm not very tall.
   If I were/was taller, I'd play basketball.

2 She can't get a job in Canada because she doesn't speak English.
   _____

3 I haven't got enough free time to learn to play a new sport.
   _____

4 I want to send Tom a message but I don't know his email address.
   _____

5 My uncle's too old to be an airline pilot.
   _____

6 I don't read very quickly because my eyesight isn't very good.
   _____

7 I'd like to buy a Mercedes car, but I haven't got enough money.
   _____